The Mystery of Frankenberg's Canadian Airman

Peter Hessel

James Lorimer & Company Ltd., Publishers
Toronto

James Lorimer & Company Ltd. acknowledges the support of the Ontario Arts Council. We acknowledge the support of the Government of Canada through the Book Publishing Industry Development Program (BPIDP) for our publishing activities. We acknowledge the support of the Canada Council for the Arts for our publishing program. We acknowledge the support of the Government of Ontario through the Ontario Media Development Corporation's Ontario Book Initiative.

Cover design: Meghan Collins

The Canada Council | Le Conseil des Arts
for the Arts | du Canada

ONTARIO ARTS COUNCIL
CONSEIL DES ARTS DE L'ONTARIO

Library and Archives Canada Cataloguing in Publication

Hessel, Peter, 1931-
    The mystery of Frankenberg's Canadian airman / Peter Hessel.

ISBN10: 1-55028-884-9
ISBN13: 978-1-55028-884-1

    1. Prisoners of war—Crimes against—Germany—Chemnitz. 2. World War, 1939-1945—Prisoners and prisons, German. 3. Prisoners of war—Canada. 4. Bombing, Aerial—Germany—Chemnitz. 5. World War, 1939-1945—Aerial operations, Canadian. 6. Hessel, Peter, 1931- I. Title.

D792.C2H48 2005   940.54'72'092   C2005-903276-6

James Lorimer & Company Ltd.,
Publishers
35 Britain Street
Toronto, Ontario
M5A 1R7
www.lorimer.ca

Distributed in the U.S. by
Casemate
2114 Darby Road
2nd floor
Havertown, PA
19083

Printed and bound in Canada.

CONTENTS

Other books by Peter Hessel:
The Evolution of a School
From Ottawa with Love
The Algonkin Tribe
Destination: Ottawa Valley
Fathering, Mothering and Kidding
The Algonkin Nation
McNab — The Township
Mighty Fine Bread and Fancy Pastry (with Cathy Boys)

I hate the drum's discordant sound.
Parading round, and round, and round:
To me it talks of ravaged plains,
And burning towns, and ruined swains,
And mangled limbs, and dying groans,
And widows' tears, and orphans' moans;
And all that Misery's hand bestows,
To fill the catalogue of human woes.

— John Scott of Amwell (1730–1783) —

One to destroy is murder by the law;
And gibbets keep the lifted hand in awe;
To murder thousands takes a specious name
— War's glorious art —
And gives immortal fame.

— Edward Young (1683–1765), *Love of Fame* —

I dedicate this book
to Canada
— My Children's Land —

ACKNOWLEDGEMENTS

Without the help of many individuals and institutions in Canada, Britain, and Germany, I would have been unable to research and write this book.

In Canada, I wish to express my sincere thanks for research assistance to Dr. Steve Harris (DND Archives, Ottawa); Gregg McCooeye (researcher at the Personnel Records Unit, Library and Archives Canada) and Johanne Neville of the Commonwealth War Graves Commission in Ottawa. Richard Koval of Sioux Lookout, Ontario has been generous in providing me with vital information leading to contacts with RCAF veterans. Other important information came from Colonel J.A.P. Bourdage of Quebec City, Quebec, Alain D'Avril in Montreal, Quebec, Fernand Lessard in Montreal, Quebec, Jim Watt in Orillia, Ontario, and Bill Tytula of the RCAF Museum in Trenton, Ontario. My very warm thanks go to RCAF Bomber Command veterans Harry Denison in North Bay, Ontario (and his daughter Jean Jamieson); Jack Dougherty in Burnstown, Ontario; John Gendron in Smiths Falls, Ontario; Bruce Gill in Westlock, Alberta; Glenn Matthews in Victoria, B.C.; Bill Mosey in Chatham, Ontario; Frank Mudry in Swift Current, Saskatchewan; Joe Parent in Kapuskasing, Ontario (and his son Tony); to Marjorie Lamontagne in Portage La Prairie, Manitoba (widow of Leo Lamontagne), and Joy Loveridge in Qualicum Beach, B.C. (widow of Doug Loveridge). I thank Randy Boswell of the *Ottawa Citizen* for his early encouragement. For their editorial guidance and improvement, I am grateful to Phil Jenkins in Chelsea, Quebec, and Pamela Martin in Thomasburg, Ontario. At James Lorimer & Company, I thank Jennifer Fox, Stacey Curtis, Jim Lorimer, and Lynn Schellenberg for their patience and cheerful collaboration. I am grateful for support received from Dominion President, Mary Ann Burdett, and Dominion Secretary, Duane Daly, of the Royal Canadian Legion's Dominion Command in Ottawa, and to Randy Whiteman and Royal Canadian Legion Branch 174 in Arnprior, Ontario.

Thanks to Michelle Borchers, Judy Cerigo, and Nicole White for French-English translations. Lise and Jean Desjardins of Montreal enabled me to continue the story. Their appreciation warmed my heart and justified my efforts. My children — Ingo, Dieter, Alexander, Duncan, and Stephanie — all took an interest in this project, encouraged me, and provided me with ideas, inspiration, and constructive criticism. Thank you, Elizabeth, for giving me strength and inspiration from beginning to end.

In Britain, I am grateful to Emily Bird and Carol Gamble of the Commonwealth War Graves Commission in Maidenhead. Alan Wells of Camborne in Cornwall helped me by scanning and e-mailing pages from Chorley's "BC Losses 1945," which I couldn't access here.

I was fortunate to have a very effective support network in Germany. Fritz Neidhardt played an active role as my research assistant. In addition, Fritz and Irmgard provided me with shelter, food, transportation, and comfort during three forays in Saxony. I would have failed in my task without Marion Rau, Archivist at the Frankenberg Municipal Archives. I thank the eyewitnesses to the murder in Frankenberg: Anni Bodenschatz, Lieselotte Braune, Ulrich Köhler, and Elfriede Rupprecht, and also Dr. Ewald Kuschka of Flöha, who remembers the deed.

I am grateful to Andreas Luksch, Frau Juntke, and Andrea Voigt, journalists at the Freie Presse. *Vielen Dank* to Dr. Ulrich Koch, who kickstarted everything; to the late Dr. Manfred Ahnert, Eberhardt Hübsch of Dresden, and Dieter Miedtank of Chemnitz for their early research; and to the "Ore Mountain Men": Herbert Berger, Lothar Ficker, Eberhard Gerlach, Achim Hartmann, Manfred Heeg, Egon Lötzsch, Kurt Melzer, Hermann Pährisch, Kurt Scheffler, Fritz Uhlig, and Gottfried Wolff. I am grateful to Joanna Brzozowska (Marienheide) for her assistance, compassion, and friendship. Other beacons on the road to discovery were Uwe Fiedler (Director of the Schlossberg Museum in Chemnitz), Wolfgang Hammer in Sachsenburg, and Willi Wachholz in Schwerte. I thank the following for understanding and supporting my efforts at reconciliation: Günter Assman (Freiberg), Elke Beer (Head Librarian, Chemnitz), Erwin Brandt (Frankenberg), Claus-D. Härtel of Chemnitz (who also provided me with valuable audiovisual material), Addi Jacobi (Chemnitz), Dietmar Palm and other members of the Historical Society in Frankenberg, Günter Rupprecht (Sachsenburg), Günter Schwab (Oberweidbach), Ursula Stopp (Ehrenfriedersdorf), Holger Uhlig (Zschopau), Nils Werner and crew (MDR TV, Dresden). For their comforting presence in Berlin, I owe thanks to Father (Maj.) Z. Gracjan Burkiciak and the following Canadian Embassy staff: Military Attaché, Navy Captain Stuart Andrews; Minister-Counsellor, Chris Greenshields; and Public Affairs Attaché, Thilo Lenz.

FOREWORD

Here's a real who dunnit for Canada's Year of the Veteran. It's about war, politics, truth, and, above all, terror, wholesale and retail, as told by a German who survived both the horrors of Nazism and the ruthless Allied bomber offensive against Germany. He then solves a shocking mystery that Canadian officials had left in the shadows.

In the last months of World War II, our Soviet allies accused their western allies of letting them carry the heaviest burden of killing and dying. Our answer was Operation Thunderclap, the annihilation of Dresden, Chemnitz, and other Saxon cities hitherto untouched. Peter Hessel was thirteen in 1945, after a war that had taken his family from Chemnitz to Poland, and finally, as refugees at the end of the war, to the little garrison town of Frankenberg. On a street not far from where he and his family lived, a young Canadian prisoner of war was beaten to death while his armed escort watched passively. Was it a spontaneous act of vengeance by civilians driven to insensate fury by the bombing, or was it orchestrated by local Nazis, fulfilling Josef Goebbels's call?

Only weeks later, American and then Soviet troops liberated Frankenberg. The Allied victory turned the murder of a helpless prisoner of war into a war crime. However, Canadian war crimes investigators soon withdrew from the case. Saxony was part of the Soviet Zone. Relations were already difficult. Perhaps they had enough to do elsewhere, including prosecuting the notorious General Kurt Meyer, whose 12th SS "Hitler Jugend" Division had killed Canadian prisoners wholesale.

Peter Hessel emigrated to Canada after the war and became a loyal citizen and public servant. Some quirk of circumstance and character persuaded him to do what his adopted country had failed to do. When he retired, he decided to seek the truth about the tragic mystery of the Canadian flyer in Frankenberg. As ignorant of our military history as most Canadians, he was shocked to discover that fellow Canadians had shared fully in Operation Thunderclap, suffering up to 40 percent of the heavy casualties, and dropping at least a third of the bombs that had devastated his hometown, leaving infants and children trapped and burning in their own homes, civilians drowning in faeces when septic tanks burst and flooded into underground shelters, and old women bleeding to death or asphyxiated beside blocked escape routes.

With impressive fortitude, ingenuity, and effort, Peter Hessel kept looking for the Canadian airman who had died alone and needlessly amidst so much other death. He was encouraged by the compassion and curiosity of both Germans and Canadians intrigued by his mystery, and repeatedly frustrated by the dead ends and blind spots of any investigation. Who was the young victim? Who were his murderers?

Official sources, here and in Germany, had no plausible answer. Nor did scores of people who knew something about the event but never enough. Despite the mounting cost and his repeated failures, Hessel somehow kept on looking.

By the end of the book, you will know the answers that Hessel found. Answers to the other and even more intriguing questions of why and how these tragedies happened and were forgotten should keep your mind working for very much longer, perhaps even forever.

Desmond Morton
Professor of History
McGill University
June 2005

CHAPTER 1

Frankenberg Spring, 1945

May 7, 1945

We had been in the cellar air-raid shelter for several days and nights. The room had no windows. Only a single light bulb dangled from the ceiling. Soon, it flickered and died. The power was off. We were in total darkness. Once in a while, someone lit a dim flashlight. Some people smoked. I saw the telltale red glimmer here and there. My mother smoked too. No one objected. It might be her last cigarette, I thought. There was an air shaft somewhere, but the air we inhaled was foul. Outside, everything was quiet, but no one dared to go outside to look. Suddenly there was a loud knock on the cellar door. A man's voice shouted in German: "You can all come out, the *Amis* are here." We ducked under the low steel beam at the shelter entrance and filed out. I had to shield my eyes from the bright sunlight. Then I took some deep breaths of fresh spring air.

"Is the war over yet?" a woman asked.

"Not yet, but it can't last much longer."

I went upstairs to change from pyjamas to a pair of corduroy shorts and a white shirt. Then I walked downtown to the market square. I expected masses of American soldiers with tanks and guns. Instead, just a handful of jeeps had pulled up in front of the town hall. Here, someone had hoisted three "enemy" flags: the Stars and Stripes, the Union Jack, and, in the middle, the Hammer and Sickle of the Soviet Union. This was the first time I had ever seen black men. They looked foreign and frightening, especially in their U.S. uniforms. Yet I was surprised by the relaxed and easygoing attitude of the soldiers. Some were lounging in open jeeps, feet dangling over the sides. Others sat on the sidewalk, smoking cigarettes, their submachine guns in front of them on the pavement. A handful of motorcycles were parked at the curb. Was this the end of the war? A soldier nailed a large poster to the main door of the town hall. The wording was in German: Everyone was ordered to bring weapons and other military gear to a collection point at the town hall. Anyone disobeying this order would get the *Todesstrafe* (death penalty). I ran all the way back to the house. I grabbed the spade and uncovered my "treasure."

A few days earlier, I had dug a deep hole in the garden behind the house and buried my shiny new flare gun and ammo, the copy of *Mein Kampf* I had won in an essay contest, my framed photo of the Führer, my Hitler Youth knife in its leather sheath, and one of my most prized possessions: my diamond-shaped sharpshooter's badge with the swastika emblem.

Now, I took out my flare gun, the ammunition box and my knife. I left the other things in the hole and hastily covered it up again. I rolled an empty rain barrel over it. My aunt handed me her husband's ceremonial officer's sabre and told me to give it to the Americans. We had no other weapons in the house.

I walked back to the market square carrying the flare gun, the knife, the sabre, and the ammunition box. I stood in an orderly queue of people holding all kinds of weapons, including some antique shotguns and pistols. A table had been set up in a hall inside the town hall. One soldier stood on each side of the table. Another, who I learned was called

Frankenberg town hall in May 1945.

a "loo-tenant," sat on a chair behind it. Finally it was my turn to surrender my weapons. The lieutenant pointed at the box I held under my arm and asked in English, "What's in there?"

Proud to have understood him, I said, "Ammunition."

"Oh, you speak English?"

"I can speak a little," I answered.

He looked inside the box and smiled when he saw the flares. He took my knife, had a good look at it, and weighed it in his hand. On the pommel it had a black swastika against a white and red diamond-shaped background.

"You in the Hitler Youth?" he asked.

"In the Jungvolk. I'm only thirteen."

"That your sword?" I didn't understand the word. "That yours?"

"No, Sir. My uncle's."

"And where's your uncle?"

"At the front. I don't know."

He reached in his pocket, pulled out a chocolate bar, broke off some pieces, and gave them to me.

"Have some American chocolate."

"Thank you, Sir," I stuttered.

That was my first English conversation outside the classroom.

It was February 2004. I had finally come to the end of my memoirs. It had taken me years to record my childhood reminiscences, going back as far as the early years of the Nazi regime in Germany, the years before the war, when I was being systematically indoctrinated into Nazi ideology. Writing about my experiences during the six war years had often caused nightmares. Now, after writing on and off for years, I decided to stop right there — at the end of World War II, in May 1945. I had already written over 300 pages. The spring of 1945 was the season when my childhood abruptly ended. I had written enough.

Yes, this was a good place to stop. However, I still wanted to tie up some loose ends. I consulted the World Wide Web to find some background information. Which German Wehrmacht unit was stationed at the huge Frankenberg barracks — minutes from where I lived? Which U.S. army unit had shelled the town with howitzer guns? Which U.S. troops had entered Frankenberg on May 7, 1945, the day before the war ended? Which Soviet unit occupied us the very next day, after the Americans had turned around and left the town to the "Russians"?

On February 22, 2004 I brought up the Yahoo browser and typed in "Frankenberg 1945." Several Web sites seemed relevant to the subject. One of them, posted by Ulrich Koch in Germany, pointed me in the right direction. I opened it and found Ernst Rossberg's recollections of "The Brief American Occupation of Parts of East Germany, 1945." The Web site included some useful information about German, U.S., and Soviet military units operating in the vicinity at the end of the war. There were a few discrepancies concerning the date and length of the American "occupation." Koch was asking for input from people who remembered those days in 1945. I e-mailed Koch to tell him I did indeed remember the Americans coming to Frankenberg in May 1945.

That evening the telephone rang in my office. The caller identified himself as Dr Ulrich Koch, a documentary filmmaker in Berlin. He had received my e-mail and wanted to talk to me about Frankenberg. He told me what his records indicated: the American unit that had held the town under fire belonged to U.S. Field Artillery Battalions 302 and 355, part of the 76th Infantry Division. (I later learned that the American soldiers who had briefly entered Frankenberg on May 7, 1945, belonged to the 2nd Battalion of U.S. Infantry Regiment 76 under Lieutenant Colonel Donald Richardson.) I happily jotted down the information. It turned out to be a long phone call. I calculated that it was after 2 a.m. in Berlin.

When I mentioned this, Dr Koch laughed and told me that he is a night owl and workaholic.

"So you live in Canada now, and you lived in Frankenberg at the end of the war — how interesting. Did you know that a Canadian airman was murdered by the SS in the streets of Frankenberg?"

No, I had never heard this.

"When?" I asked.

"Right at the end of the war. I'll look it up and send you some information about it. I think he was buried as an unknown Canadian."

"How did a Canadian end up in Frankenberg?"

"You said you were born in Chemnitz. Surely you must know that Canadians played a major part in the destruction of your city?"

"No," I said. I found that difficult to believe. "I had no idea. I thought it was the British at night and the Americans in the day-time. I know, of course, that some Canadians were flying with the RAF. Is that what you mean?"

"No. I mean that the Royal Canadian Air Force actually flew Canadian planes from Canadian bases in Britain. They had several squadrons over Chemnitz as well as over Dresden. In March, one of their bombers crashed near Chemnitz. A Canadian air-man apparently bailed out, was captured in Frankenberg, and murdered by the SS."

This aroused my curiosity. I had never heard of anything or anybody Canadian when I lived in Frankenberg as a young teenager.

Frankenberg is a small town in hilly country on the Zschopau, a little river that tumbles down from the nearby Ore Mountains. In 1945, the town had about 16,000 inhabitants. In addition, it was harbouring several thousand refugees from the east, includ-ing my mother, sister, and me, who had fled from the rapidly advancing, avenging Red Army.

My mother, my sister, and I had lived in Kalisz, in occupied

"I thought it was the British and the Americans ..." Chemnitz after the bombing of March 5/6, 1945.

Poland, since 1942. Kalisz was in a region that had been annexed to the Grossdeutsches Reich (Great German Empire) and renamed Wartheland. Hitler's plan had been to "Germanize" the entire region. My mother followed the call to go east. Once established there, she moved our entire household from Chemnitz to Poland. In Kalisz, I went to a German grammar school and served in the junior branch of the Hitler Youth, the Jungvolk. Then, in January 1945, we were forced to flee, leaving all our possessions behind except for what we could squeeze into four suitcases. We slowly moved west in a long refugee trek before we finally ended up living with my aunt in Frankenberg.

Apart from housing all these eastern refugees, Frankenberg had also given shelter to evacuees from Chemnitz, just fifteen kilometres to the west. Chemnitz, a heavily industrialized city, normally had a population of 350,000. The city had been bombed several times in February 1945, and again on March 3, before it was largely destroyed in a firestorm triggered by massive

Allied air raids on March 5 and 6. Chemnitz was where I was born and had spent the first ten years of my life. Frankenberg was our temporary place of refuge.

After speaking with Koch, I looked up a few Web sites and found some facts and figures that surprised me. It was absolutely true: Canadians *had* played a significant role in the destruction of my hometown! And a Canadian was supposed to have been murdered in Frankenberg? I found it difficult to sleep that night. Visions of March 1945 spun around in my head.

The next day I decided to look into the case. I felt a strong urge to know the story of this murder. I felt that it was deeply connected to my own story. After all, I thought, I am probably the only person in the world whose hometown is Chemnitz, the airman's target; who lived in Frankenberg at the time of the murder; and who became a Canadian. I believed I was in a unique position. Maybe I could write an article about it.

In the beginning, I had several goals. Koch had said that the Canadian airman was unidentified, so my first objective was to identify him. I wanted to discover his name and learn something about the circumstances of his death. I wanted to find his burial place and perhaps provide some comfort to any surviving family members. Gradually, my project gathered its own momentum. I widened my approach. From the start, the case had presented itself to me as a mystery in reverse. My challenge was not to discover the perpetrators of a crime, but its victim.

I remembered my mother's diaries, which I had acquired after she died in 1983. Would she have mentioned the murder in Frankenberg? Although I had never heard of it, I thought it likely that she had. I found her record of 1945. What she kept was not really a personal, intimate diary, but only a daily journal in a calendar called *Geschäfts-Tagebuch 1945*, printed on very poor wartime paper and crudely stitched.

When I opened the pages to early March 1945, I was disappointed by the extreme brevity of her entries. Surely she must have recognized the magnitude of the events, the end of the Third Reich and World War II, to which she was a witness? Of course, her main concern was her immediate family. And yet, it would have been so enlightening to know what thoughts and feelings she had at the time. Whatever they were, she did not express them in her diary. Nor did she mention the murder of a Canadian airman in Frankenberg. Either she hadn't heard of it, or she considered the death of one man — and an enemy soldier at that — too trivial to record at a time when thousands were dying every day, all over Germany.

Two days after Dr Koch's phone call, I contacted Dr Steve Harris at the Directory of History and Heritage, Department of National Defence in Ottawa and asked if he had any information about this murder of a Canadian airman. He invited me to come and see the archives on Holly Lane, housed in an unassuming building in a very uninteresting part of the capital. There I found not only documents about the participation of the Royal Canadian Air Force (RCAF) in the destruction of my hometown, Chemnitz, but also a file containing a copy of a fascinating report.[1]

It had been submitted to the Canadian Defence Headquarters on March 30, 1946, by a body with a very long-winded name: "Canadian War Crimes Investigation Unit on Miscellaneous War Crimes against members of Canadian Armed Forces in the European Theatre of Operation, 9 September 1939 to 8 May 1945," also known as the CWCIU.[2] The unit was established right after the war and only had a short life. It concerned itself mainly with the prosecution of SS *Brigadeführer* Kurt Meyer, who was held responsible for the execution of Canadian soldiers in Normandy. The report described the case of a murder in Frankenberg, as it had been reported to the Canadian unit by the British War Crimes Section on September 8, 1945.

Under "Origin, Statement of Atrocity and Investigation," the unit's commanding officer, Lt.Col B.J.S. MacDonald, stated: "[The case] concerns the murder of an unidentified Canadian airman by German civilians. It has been impossible to start an investigation as scene of crime is in the Russian zone."

According to the document:

Some time during the early part of April, a Canadian aviator parachuted from his plane at Frankenberg, Germany. After his capture he was placed in custody of the IV Veterinary Reserve and Training Division in Frankenberg. Five soldiers of the 2nd Company of this Division, disguised as civilians, attacked and allegedly beat the victim to death, as he was being taken to the railway station of that city. The victim was buried in the cemetery at Frankenberg.

The information in the report came to the British authorities from Alfred Hermann Paul of Leipzig, who "did not see the crime committed but on the same day saw the body which had a completely broken skull." Paul also provided the name of another possible witness, a Dr Katz (also spelled "Kaatz" in the report), but apparently neither the British section nor the Canadian unit took any steps to find him. Nor, it seems, did anyone from the British section actually travel to Frankenberg to interview witnesses. Certainly the Canadian investigating officers never did.

Under "Disposition," the report concludes: "Inasmuch as the scene of the alleged crime and the witnesses are all in the Russian zone of occupied Germany, the investigation has been delayed until authority to enter that zone can be obtained." This conclusion does not seem entirely justified. There is evidence that American and British military personnel were allowed to travel in the Soviet-occupied zone of Germany until 1948, when the Cold War began to flare up. For example, as late as December 1948, a British unit was allowed to exhume the graves of British and Canadian soldiers in Saxony and other areas of East Germany and transfer the bodies to British cemeteries. It is quite likely that if the British section or the Canadian unit had pursued the matter, the Soviet authorities would have allowed an investigation to proceed.

I found the date in the report ("during the early part of April") to be inconsistent with what Dr Koch had told me, that the Canadian had been murdered on the day after the major Bomber Command air raid on Chemnitz, March 6, 1945. Also inconsistent was the allegation that the murder had been committed by "soldiers disguised as civilians," rather than by the SS, as Dr Koch had said. Later, I was also able to determine that the unit stationed in Frankenberg was not a division, as described in the report, but an *Abteilung* (a unit of only battalion strength).

Frankenberg had been an important garrison town since the early eighteenth century. One year before the outbreak of World War I, construction of a large compound called "*die Kaserne*" (the barracks) began. By July 1914, 18 substantial buildings had been completed. Construction continued until 1917, partly with the help of 400 prisoners of war. At that time, the barracks housed various infantry, artillery, and officer training units. After the Treaty of Versailles reduced Germany's armed forces to 100,000 men, the Frankenberg garrison, too, was reduced to skeleton strength. When Hitler began to rearm, the barracks were initially occupied by a heavy artillery regiment. From 1936 to 1937, they also housed the 3rd Battalion of the SS Death Head Division, called Sachsen (Saxony), which supplied guards for the nearby Sachsenburg concentration camp. In 1940, the artillery regiment was re-formed as a reserve and training battalion.

The reason I lived in Frankenberg from February 1945 to June 1946 was indirectly connected with the barracks. My Uncle Hans had just graduated as a veterinarian when the war broke out. He was immediately drafted into the Wehrmacht as a veterinary officer and given the rank of second lieutenant. In 1941, he married my mother's youngest sister, Trautel. Hans was then posted to Frankenberg where, by this time, the barracks included extensive stables housing many horses. The veterinarians were attached to a unit, called "*Fahnenschmiede*" (military blacksmiths), that provided veterinary care for the horses. So the 1945–46 British/Canadian war crimes investigation report was right that the battalion had a veterinary component.

When I left the DND archives after my first visit, I was glad to have found a lot of information about Canada's contribution to Bomber Command. I had also learned much about the air raid against Chemnitz on February 13/14, 1945, and collected some material about the massive attack on March 5/6, 1945, which dwarfed all previous bombing raids on Chemnitz. Best of all, I had discovered official acknowledgement in Canadian military files of the murder of a Canadian airman in Frankenberg. But I was very disappointed to find neither the name of the victim nor specific details of the crime.

In spite of its apparent inaccuracies, the CWCIU report left no doubt: someone in Frankenberg had known and reported that a Canadian airman was killed shortly before the end of the war. The murder had come to the attention of Canadian military officials. But then the case was simply filed away. The Canadian military and the government allowed this murder of a Canadian prisoner of war to be forgotten.

Later, I learned from records at Library and Archives Canada that the CWCIU had been established on June 4, 1945, less than a month after the end of the war in Europe. The Frankenberg murder is mentioned only once in the unit's "Secret War Diaries," and the town's name is misspelled at that: On September 14, 1945, a brief entry reads: "FRANKENBURG case reported to unit Head Quarters." Perhaps due to the rapidly changing political climate, the unit had only a short life. It was disbanded less than a year after it was established. The last entry, on May 22, 1946, reads: "All files and equipment having been turned in and accounted for, the Unit ceased to function as a War Crimes Investigation Unit."

My task seemed overwhelmingly difficult. Even the British and Canadian military had given up their investigation and closed the file. I inquired whether the War Crimes Section of the Department of Justice Canada — with its sizeable budget — might wish to look into the case. After all, the victim was a Canadian, and a war crime had been committed. However, I was barking up the wrong tree. The War Crimes Section was established in 1987 in response to the report of the Deschênes Commission of Inquiry on War Criminals, which had been presented to the House of Commons the previous year. The Section is still functioning. However, the investigation of crimes against members of the Canadian armed forces during World War II does not form part of its mandate, which is the investigation and prosecution of alleged war criminals now residing in Canada.[3]

CHAPTER 2

Operation Thunderclap

aving spent 52 years of my life in Canada, I knew, of course, that some Canadian airmen had seen service over Germany. Back in the 1980s, I read *Terror in the Starboard Seat*[1] by my good friend, the late Dave McIntosh, Canadian Press correspondent and later publishing director of the National Capital Commission in Ottawa. When Dave autographed a copy of his book for me, he was somewhat taken aback when I asked him, "What exactly do you mean by terror, Dave? The terror you *felt* or the terror you *delivered*?"

Now that I knew that Canadians had been involved in the bombing of my hometown, Chemnitz, I was motivated to learn more about Bomber Command, the operation code-named Thunderclap, and Canada's participation in both.

In 1936, the Royal Air Force (RAF) was reorganized into six functional commands. Bomber Command was the name given to the high command of all British bomber units. Early in World War II, squadrons from the Canadian, Australian, New Zealand, and other

Commonwealth forces were integrated into Bomber Command, which from February 1942 to the end of the war was headed by Air Vice Marshal Arthur T. Harris. Although Canadians flew with Bomber Command from the outbreak of war, Canadian involvement grew dramatically as the war progressed. Canada was also host to the British Commonwealth Air Training Plan, which produced a total of 131,553 Australian, British, Canadian and New Zealand aircrew. Of the graduates, 72,835 were RCAF pilots, navigators, bomb aimers, wireless operators/air gunners, air gunners, and flight engineers.

By 1944, Bomber Command had seven operational groups. Five of them, Groups One, Three, Four, Five, and Six, were the bomber groups. Six Group, the largest, was made up of 15 RCAF squadrons, each with 18 to 25 heavy bombers.[2] When Six Group was created in October 1942, it was staffed largely by Canadians. By early 1944, up to a third of Six Group personnel came from other Commonwealth forces. By then, more Canadians were flying in RAF groups than in Six Group.

Even Josef Goebbels, Hitler's Minister for People's Enlightenment and Propaganda, took note of Canada's contribution to Bomber Command. From his diaries:

> It drives me mad to think some Canadian boor, who probably can't even find Europe on the globe, flies here from a country glutted with natural resources, which they don't know how to exploit, to bombard a continent with a crowded population.[3]

The Canadian effort within Bomber Command reached its peak in 1944 when Six Group flew 25,353 sorties. Six Group flew a total of almost 41,000 missions during the war. Its airmen clocked 271,981 hours and dropped 126,122 tons of bombs — almost one-eighth of the total tonnage dropped by Bomber Command. The bombs delivered by Six Group accounted for a large portion of the nearly 600,000 dead and 675,000 wounded Germans on the ground. In its 30 months of operations, Six Group lost 814 aircraft, and 3,500 of its airmen were killed. Another 4,700 Canadians died while serving with other Bomber Command groups. Canadian crews were awarded 8,000 decorations for bravery.[4]

> Our expansion was greatly helped by the Royal Canadian Air Force, which provided a whole group, No. 6 Group of Bomber Command, on January 1st, 1943, as well as other squadrons outside its own Group. The Canadian Government paid the whole cost of this Group and of all the R.C.A.F.'s operational squadrons, including the cost of the fuel and ammunition they used, out of Canadian taxes and domestic loans. In January 1943, 37 per cent of the pilots in Bomber Command belonged to the Dominion and Colonial Air Forces, and of these 60 per cent were Canadian.[5]

It may come as a surprise to many that far more Canadians were killed in Bomber Command than in the Dieppe raid and on D-Day combined. The two latter events have been widely covered by the Canadian media, while this country's contribution to Bomber Command has not. During the disastrous Dieppe raid (code-named Operation Jubilee) on August 19, 1942, slightly more than 900 Canadian soldiers died, and 1,874 were taken prisoner. The RCAF lost 13 planes and 10 pilots at Dieppe.[6] On D-Day, June 6, 1944 (the beginning of the Normandy invasion — Operation Overlord), 340 of the 21,400 landed Canadian soldiers died and 47 were taken prisoner. Throughout the entire Normandy campaign, 5,020 Canadian soldiers died.[7] However, the media have been very silent about the fact that almost 10,000 Canadian airmen lost their lives in Bomber Command. Of course, the Dieppe and D-Day losses each occurred in a single day and the Normandy losses in a little over two months, while the Bomber Command losses apply to the entire war. No one should try to belittle Canada's sacrifices on land and at sea. On the other hand, the extent of Canadian Bomber Command casualties deserves to be better known. It seems that the media have neglected to recognize and commemorate the sacrifice of so many young Canadian airmen. Perhaps journalists are simply unaware of the scale. The controversy surrounding strategic bombing of civilian targets has probably been a factor as well. Perhaps the Canadian public doesn't want to see its war heroes depicted as killers of women and children. Yet knowledge of the truth is the first step to understanding.

By the beginning of 1945, after the success of the Allied landings in France and the rapid Soviet advances in the east, it had become evident that World War II in Europe would be over soon. The principle on which the Allied leadership was operating was this: the faster the Nazi government could be brought to its knees, the fewer Allied soldiers would have to die on both fronts. And it was believed that undermining civilian morale would be an effective tool in achieving this goal. Some argue that bloody vengeance was also on the minds of the men who planned the grand finale. No doubt that is true as well. Of course, German cities had been continuously hammered by the 8th U.S. Army Air Force and Bomber Command from as early as 1941. Now, however, an even more powerful blow was being envisaged. With the greatest concentration of air power and airborne explosives the world had ever seen, the stage was set for Armageddon.

On the night of January 25, 1945, British Prime Minister Winston Churchill asked Sir Archibald Sinclair, the Secretary for Air, what plans the RAF had for "basting the Germans in their retreat from Breslau." Sinclair replied that air operations along those lines were now being considered. However, Churchill was not satisfied. He wanted a demonstration to counteract Stalin's claim that the British and Americans had slowed down and were leaving the lion's share of the fighting to the Red Army. As a result of Churchill's impatience, on January 27, 1945, Air Marshal Sir Norman Bottomley instructed the man in charge of Bomber Command, Air Vice Marshal Sir Arthur Harris ("Bomber Harris"), to put Operation Thunderclap into effect.[8]

The code name *Thunderclap* had originally been coined by the British Joint Intelligence Committee (JIC) in July 1944, shortly after the failed attempt on Hitler's life. A massive air attack on Berlin was to flatten the already heavily damaged city. The plan had envisaged 220,000 civilian casualties in the hope that this would have a "shattering effect on political and civilian morale all over Germany."[9] The scheme was temporarily shelved, to be resurrected again in January 1945, but — for military and political reasons — with different targets. Now, the clearly stated intention was to lend assistance to the Red Army on the eastern front. Following Churchill's and Bottomley's instructions, Harris suggested that Magdeburg, Chemnitz, Leipzig, Dresden, and other cities near the eastern front should be attacked "where a severe blitz will not only cause confusion in the evacuation from the East but will also hamper the movement of [German] troops from the West."[10] Churchill agreed. With his encouragement, the Air Ministry ordered that Thunderclap be carried out. The plan was coordinated with the Americans and implemented over the next few months.[11]

The story of the major bombing raids on Dresden is well-known throughout the world. *Dresden* has become a household word, a synonym for the ruthless annihilation of civilians and the barbaric destruction of cultural heritage. At 13, I was an eyewitness to the destruction of Dresden — from a distance of some 80 kilometres. The following excerpt from my memoirs paints an image I will never forget.

February 1945
In the evening of Shrove Tuesday, February 13, the sirens wailed again. We were so used to air-raid alerts that we no longer headed straight for the shelter. Instead, we turned on

the radio and tuned it to the wire broadcast. We knew we were tuned to it when we heard its constant ticking sound. Every few minutes, the ticking was interrupted by a voice message, such as: "*Achtung! Achtung!* Here is a *Drahtfunk* announcement. A large enemy bomber formation with fighter escort is approaching the Hannover and Braunschweig airspace, on a southeasterly course." We were concerned mostly with the bombers heading for our area. At that point, we turned the dial to the *Polizeifunk*, a short-wave police broadcast in Chemnitz. It announced that the reported bomber formation was now approaching the Halle/Leipzig airspace and that it was followed by another large formation holding the same course. We knew something big was coming our way. We gathered the whole family and prepared to go down to the shelter. I took the radio with me.

Now the *Polizeifunk* reported that one formation after another was operating over Dresden. This was unexpected. While the Allies laid waste to city after city all across Germany, rumour had it that they would spare Dresden, not only because it was declared a "hospital city" (it had about 20 large hospitals), but also because of its world-famous architecture and art treasures, and because it had virtually no heavy industry. I pictured the scenes in the homes and public buildings and packed streets of the city where we ourselves had been refugees less than three weeks earlier. When we realized that the Chemnitz area was not under direct attack, we ventured outside into the starry, frosty night. The eastern horizon was coloured a deep red, reflecting the firestorms raging in Dresden. In the morning, we heard that the entire central part of the city was a sea of fire, with hundreds of thousands presumed dead and dying. During the day, as the wounded and burned humanity struggled for survival, more bomber formations attacked Dresden, turning it into a mass grave of gigantic propor-

Dresden — one of many German cities destroyed by Allied saturation bombing near the end of World War II.

tions. When the inferno died down, it was announced that Dresden — "the Florence of Germany" — no longer existed.

But perhaps the story of this particular attack has become

more famous, or infamous, than it deserves. I have encountered many Canadians who — until I told them otherwise — believed that Dresden was the only German city destroyed by Allied air raids. It was only one of many. In fact, had the Allies not destroyed Dresden, it would have been the only major city in Germany to escape their wrath. Civilian casualties in Hamburg, for example, were much higher than those in Dresden.

Dresden also did not culminate Allied strategic bombing of Germany. While the atomic bombs dropped in short succession on Hiroshima and Nagasaki ended the war with Japan, the catastrophic fire bombing of Dresden did not end anything. On the contrary, in March 1945 — the month following the big Dresden raid — Bomber Command dropped more than 67,000 tons of bombs on what was left of Germany, the greatest tonnage of any single month during the war. This was just slightly less than the entire tonnage dropped during the first three years of the war.

Irreplaceable cultural treasures were destroyed in all German cities and towns under attack. Great architectural and artistic heritage was also wiped out in German air attacks on Guernica, Warsaw, Rotterdam, London, Coventry, etc. If in its attack on the centre of Coventry on November 14/15, 1940, the Luftwaffe had been able to deploy the destructive force of 1,000 heavy bombers instead of "only" 437 aircraft, the result would have been a firestorm as well. Instead of some 500, there would have been tens of thousands of civilian deaths in that city. Nevertheless, with morbid sarcasm, Nazi propaganda minister Goebbels boasted of the Luftwaffe's success in that 1940 air raid and coined the diabolical term *coventrieren* (to devastate a city in the fashion of Coventry).

Not many Canadians have ever heard of Chemnitz, let alone its destruction shortly before the end of World War II. Chemnitz had its beginnings more than 900 years ago. During the Industrial Revolution, the small Saxon town very rapidly grew into a major city. During the Communist regime of the German Democratic Republic, the name was changed to Karl-Marx-Stadt, but by 1990, it was back to its original. The city hasn't made many headlines, either as Chemnitz or as Karl-Marx-Stadt, and it has never been a tourist attraction. At best, it is worth a footnote in travel guides of Saxony.

Even as a native Chemnitzer, as a Canadian resident and citizen for five decades, I certainly had no idea that its destruction had any Canadian content. I had always taken it for granted that British and U.S. bombers had destroyed my hometown. Yet, at the DND archives I discovered that approximately 25 percent of the bomber force that caused the big firestorm in Chemnitz on March 5, 1945, was Canadian. The RCAF was indeed an awesome force during World War II.

> From a prewar strength of a few thousand men and a handful of obsolete aircraft, this force grew to become the world's fourth largest, as Canada's enemies lay prostrate. The major fighting element of the RCAF was No. 6 Group, the largest in Bomber Command.[12]

At the DND archives, I found detailed written and photographic records of two major bombing missions against Chemnitz in 1945, in which the RCAF played a role. Both attacks had been part of the operation Thunderclap — as were the raids that destroyed Dresden, Leipzig, Halle, Magdeburg, and other eastern German cities. Bomber Command and the 3rd Air Division of the 8th U.S. Army Air Force planned a major operation against Chemnitz for February 14/15, 1945.[13]

> If it succeeded, the raid would complete not just the annihilation of two important cities, but it would wipe out the entire industrial, transport and communication system of eastern Saxony, just as the Soviets were approaching. The defending Germans would have their backs to a wasteland … Chemnitz was crammed with refugees, many of whom had escaped from Dresden.[14]

At Library and Archives Canada, I found maps precisely out-lining the plans for Bomber Command operations in the night of February 14/15, 1945. The main thrust of the attack, to be flown in two phases, was against Chemnitz, "the primary target." The first phase was over Chemnitz from 8:51 to 9:21 p.m., the second phase from 12:21 to 12:59 a.m.[15]

The raid was scheduled to begin less than 48 hours after the destruction of Dresden. It was not the first time Chemnitz had been attacked by bombers. Raids on sections of the city had taken place on May 12, June 29, and September 11, 1944. On February 6, 1945, the 8th U.S. Army Air Force had dropped 800 tons of bombs on Chemnitz when bad weather forced a diversion from the primary objective, a precision attack on oil targets. I remember that date well, because that is when my grandmother's house in the suburb of Furth was destroyed by a bomb and seven people across the street were killed. The Civic Hospital was hit, and eight patients, all for-eign nationals, were killed. However, the attacks of February 14/15 were the first major operation with Chemnitz as the prime target. According to some accounts, the Allies considered it a failure.

The 8th U.S. Army Air Force attacked the city during the day on February 14. However, only about a third of its 441 bombers ear-marked for Chemnitz actually found the target. The other aircraft had to bomb alternate cities (Bamberg and Eger). Bomber Com-mand, on the other hand, had committed 717 planes (including 118 RCAF planes from Six Group) to the night raids that followed the American daytime attack. The first wave, approximately 350 RAF and RCAF aircraft, arrived over Chemnitz at 8:51 p.m. A dense cloud cover protected the city. In this phase, the downtown area suffered relatively little damage. After midnight, when the second wave of 350 bombers arrived, they encountered zero visi-bility, and the entire operation turned out to be a fiasco for Bomber Command. Most of the bombs landed in open country. The Canadian contingent dropped 431,000 pounds of incendi-aries and 291,000 pounds of high explosives that night.

Chemnitz, instead of suffering a crushing hammer blow similar to that inflicted on Dresden, had ... escaped almost without a scratch.[16]

However, according to the Bomber Command Interpretations, the raid of February 14/15 was still considered worthwhile.[17] Photos taken by observers and evaluated by the RCAF immediately after the return of the bombers to their bases show that major damage was caused to industrial installations as well as to some residential districts. The immediate interpretation report indicated that "scattered items of damage" were seen in all parts of the city, but that there were no "large areas of devastation" anywhere. It also stated that southeast and west of the city, large concentrations of craters were observed in open fields and among lightly built-up areas. A major target, the extensive rail facilities and marshalling yards in Chemnitz, remained undamaged and "fully serviceable" with the exception of "some damage to one building" in the railway workshops.

Some factories in the southern outskirts were damaged, including the Schubert & Salzer foundry. The report did not mention that the Civic Hospital was hit for the second time. Nine German patients and seven foreign patients were killed. Two more patients were killed when another hospital, the Elisabeth Clinic, was hit.

Thanks to a very elaborate and successful diversion plan, casualties among Allied bomber crews were kept at a minimum. Most German night fighters were dispatched to the feint targets and were thus kept away from the force's main target, Chemnitz. Bomber Command losses were 20 aircraft that night, including eleven in the attack on Chemnitz. Of these eleven, six were shot down by German fighters, two by flak, and three crashed due to other causes. Four of the losses were Canadian from Six Group: Squadrons 427, 432, and 434 each lost one bomber over Germany, while a Halifax from 420 Squadron crashed on landing in England after it had to abandon the mission.[18]

The overall cost of strategic bombing in Germany was extremely high on both sides. Bomber Command lost 7,449 bombers, 47,130 aircrew were killed during operations, and over 8,000 were killed in training accidents and non-operational flights. This means that 10 percent of all British and Commonwealth fatalities in World War II were sustained by Bomber Command. The 8th U.S. Army Air Force lost 8,067 of its heavy bombers. These numbers do not include Allied fighter escorts and their crews. In the first six months of 1944 alone, the German Luftwaffe lost 2,012 fighter aircraft and 1,291 aircrew. Seventy German cities were devastated by air attacks. The 500,000 bombs that rained on Germany caused between 500,000 and 600,000 deaths and destroyed more than 3.5 million homes, leaving about 7.5 million civilians homeless.[18] The Allied air war against Germany was by far the most destructive bombardment in the history of the world.

CHAPTER 3

On the Denison Trail

Early in March 2004, I received an e-mail with a long attachment from Dr Koch containing a typescript written in 2001 by Dr Manfred Ahnert of Frankenberg entitled "The Death of the Downed Canadian Bomber Pilot in Frankenberg." Koch told me that he had found it in the Frankenberg Municipal Archives two years earlier. He also informed me, sadly, that the author had just recently died.

Ahnert was a few years younger than I and had grown up in Frankenberg. In his later years, he became one of several local amateur historians who chronicled the town's history during the Nazi period and the post-war years. Ahnert had no personal knowledge of the Frankenberg murder. He had heard local rumours of the incident and decided to investigate. Among the sources he named in his article were two German amateur military historians: Dieter Miedtank of Dresden and Eberhard Hübsch of Chemnitz. They, too, had looked at records in the Frankenberg archives and consulted some available Canadian and British Web sites concerning bomber losses. They had also spoken to some eyewitnesses whose recollections they recorded and passed on to Ahnert. The conclusions reached by Ahnert, Miedtank, and Hübsch can be summarized as follows:

In the bombing raid on Chemnitz during the night of March 5/6, 1945, an RCAF Halifax bomber, *NP-799* from 426 (Thunderbird) Squadron, was shot down by German night fighters and crashed near Frankenberg. All crew members were killed except for RCAF Flight Sergeant R.B. Denison, who survived after bailing out. As a prisoner of war, he was taken to the army barracks in Frankenberg. The next day, on March 6, while being escorted to the railway station, he was ambushed by several men and beaten to death.

Of course, I welcomed this information as a major break-through in my search. I now had the victim's name: R.B. Denison. I immediately turned to the World Wide Web and called up the site for Canada's *Book of Remembrance*, a record which includes the names of all Canadian soldiers who died in World War II. The original *Book of Remembrance* — written in beautiful calligraphy — is on display in the Memorial Chamber of the Peace Tower in the Centre Block of Canada's Parliament Buildings in Ottawa. The Web site is posted by the Department of Veterans Affairs. I thought it would only be a matter of routine now to confirm that R.B. Denison was indeed listed and to find out more about him. To my surprise and disappointment, his name was not there.

I consulted a German Web site, *Flieger-Lynchmorde im Zweiten Weltkrieg* (www.flieger-lynchmorde.de), posted by an amateur historian, that listed a large number of Allied airmen, including many Canadians, who had been murdered in Germany and Nazi-occupied countries. This Web site seemed to confirm Ahnert's account because it showed that RCAF Flight Sergeant R.B. Denison had been murdered in Frankenberg on March 6, 1945. But it gave Ahnert's typescript in the Frankenberg archives as the source. I contacted the author of the site, Willi Wachholz, and asked him if he had any other sources for this information. All he could do was to refer me to Miedtank and Hübsch, the two German military historians upon whose findings Ahnert had based his paper. Wachholz had simply copied their information about the Frankenberg murder, included it in his list, and thus made this unconfirmed information available on the World Wide Web. I did not verify the accuracy of the other cases reported by Wachholz.

I consulted a number of Web sites, hoping to find more information. One, dedicated to Six Group (www.rcaf.com/6group), had been posted by a man called Richard Koval. It showed that a Flight Sergeant W. Denison (not R.B. Denison) had been taken prisoner after his bomber, Halifax *NP-799*, coded *OW-J* (piloted by Flight Lieutenant Jack Kirkpatrick of Red Deer, Alberta), had failed to return from the bombing mission against Chemnitz on March 5/6, 1945. The other six crew members had been killed when their plane was shot down by a night fighter. I assumed that in spite of the different initials, this had to be the same Denison whom Miedtank and Hübsch had identified as the murder victim. In fact, I immediately suspected that this Canadian Web site had been the source of Miedtank's and Hübsch's information, and that they had simply recorded the wrong initials. In addition, it seemed that they had assumed, without verification, that this particular plane had crashed in the vicinity of Chemnitz and Frankenberg. I imagine they thought because the murder victim was being transported alone, that is, taken alone to the railway station that day in Frankenberg, it was reasonable to assume that he had been captured alone, and that he was captured alone because he was the sole survivor of his crew. At first, this assumption also seemed perfectly logical to me: a Canadian bomber had crashed near Chemnitz with a sole survivor. It was tempting to look no farther. But as a journalist, I have learned that it pays to verify all facts. I again checked the *Book of Remembrance*, this time looking for W. Denison. There was no entry for that name either. In fact, the book does not include any RCAF airman called Denison who died in 1945.

In April I located and telephoned Dieter Miedtank in Dresden and Eberhard Hübsch in Chemnitz. They were greatly surprised and somewhat embarrassed when I told them that I found no evidence in the *Book of Remembrance* that an R.B. Denison or a W. Denison or any Denison at all had died in 1945. They finally confirmed that they had indeed based their conclusion about the identity of the murder victim solely on Richard Koval's Web site. They couldn't tell me how the wrong initials were ever attributed to Denison.

I visited the Ottawa office of the Commonwealth War Graves Commission on Slater Street in Ottawa. There, the friendly staff provided me with a printout of all RCAF personnel who died on or about March 6, 1945. There was no entry for anyone called Denison. I also consulted *They Shall Grow Not Old*, a book that lists "over 18,000 airmen, airwomen and other nationals wearing the uniform of the RCAF, who lost their lives between September 3, 1939 and August 12, 1945." The book includes no one named Denison who died in 1945.

At Library and Archives Canada, the personnel files of RCAF members who died in World War II are available to researchers. I requested such a file for either R.B. or W. Denison or any other Denison within the time frame. No such file could be found. However, thanks to Koval's Web site, I now had the names of the other crew members from Denison's bomber. Naturally, I requested their personnel files at the archives. Within 48 hours, I received all except one, the file of Sergeant I. Giles, who was not RCAF, but RAF (a Scotsman flying with an RCAF squadron). From the files of the pilot, Flight Lieutenant Jack Kirkpatrick (of Red Deer, Alberta), Flying Officer R. Fennell (of Toronto), Flying Officer R. Stillinger (of Norwood, Manitoba), Pilot Officer J. Larson (of Montreal), and Pilot Officer R. Gunderson (of Meadow

Lake, Saskatchewan), I soon learned that the plane had indeed crashed en route to Chemnitz on March 5, 1945, but nowhere near Frankenberg or Chemnitz. Their Halifax bomber had come down with its full bomb load near the small town of Wippra in the eastern Harz Mountains. Wippra is about 250 kilometres west of Chemnitz as the crow flies. Could Denison have ended up in the Frankenberg army barracks on March 6 if he had bailed out in the Harz Mountains on March 5? It seemed highly unlikely.

From the individual documents in the files of the dead crew members, I learned an astonishing fact. Not only had the sole survivor of this crash, RCAF Flight Sergeant W.H. Denison (of Lumby, British Columbia), never been murdered, but he was safely "repatriated" to Canada after his brief sojourn as a prisoner of war in Germany.[1] No wonder I couldn't find Denison's name in the *Book of Remembrance* or anywhere else. He was a survivor of World War II, not a casualty.

On the Internet, I looked up Lumby, a village in the Okanagan Valley of British Columbia. I made some phone calls trying to find someone there who had heard of W. Denison. I had no luck. Although it was now certain that Denison had not been the murder victim, I felt compelled to track him down.

I now contacted the author of the Six Group Web site, Richard Koval. He promptly answered by e-mail, and we have had many telephone conversations since. Richard is an amazing man. He lives in Sioux Lookout, Ontario, and works as a driver for an oil company. His hobby or passion — the history of aircraft — led him to research Canada's participation in Bomber Command. He told me that he has compiled information from many sources to produce his Web site. He has access to some old records showing the 1945 addresses of RCAF crew members who returned to Canada after the war. Of course, many of these addresses are now out of date. Nevertheless, I wondered whether he might help me to find W. Denison, the lucky sole survivor of the unfortunate Halifax. I told Richard that I had tried and failed to locate Denison in Lumby. A few days later, Richard called me again. Incredibly, he had found a recent address for William Henry (Harry) Denison near North Bay, Ontario. I couldn't believe this stroke of luck. Richard had even dug up his telephone number. Could he still be alive?

I immediately called the number, and when Harry Denison answered, it was as if a window had suddenly opened on the distant past. Harry is alive and well! He confirmed that he had indeed been posted to the RCAF 426 (Thunderbird) Squadron based at Linton-on-Ouse in 1945. Yes, he had been a crew member in Halifax VII *NP-799*, coded *OW-J*, piloted by Flight Lieutenant Jack Kirkpatrick. He laughed when I told him that German Web sites and printed sources had been and still were showing that he was murdered in Frankenberg. Of course, Denison had never heard of Frankenberg. But, he told me, he had been lucky all his life.

"I was supposed to die that night when my plane crashed, but I didn't," he said dryly. As the 20-year-old tail gunner of the Halifax, he lost consciousness as the big bomber hit the ground. The Germans found him injured but alive in the wreckage. He had suffered a broken rib and some other minor injuries. He told me all he remembers:

Suddenly there was a bump, and I blacked out. When I came to, I was hanging on to the sides of the fuselage, with my feet still partly in the wrecked turret. I turned over and was very sick for a long time. My face was covered with blood. Snow drifting through the broken fuselage almost covered my body. I finally crawled out, hoping to find other members of the crew. There was not a trace of my mates. Only one foot remained of the port wing, and six feet of the starboard wing. And only the middle section of the fuselage was left.

Denison believes that his plane collided with another in mid-air

RCAF veteran William Henry
(Harry) Denison, 1999.

while en route to Chemnitz. He told me he had always been under the impression that his bomber had crashed in the Black Forest. Perhaps this was because the Harz Mountains are densely covered with very dark, mostly coniferous forests; but they are hundreds of kilometres away from the mountain range in southwestern Germany called the Black Forest.

When he recovered, he crawled out of the wreckage and made his way out of the forest. He walked along a road to a stream, from which he tried to drink. But he collapsed and was finally found by two Russian workers who carried him to a German army post. He spent a month in a German hospital in Dr Martin Luther's birthplace, the town of Eisleben, before he was transferred to a POW camp. He was never anywhere near Chemnitz or Frankenberg.

On a postcard he wrote on April 20, 1945, from Stalag VII A, he told his parents in Lumby, B.C., not to worry, that he was well and would be "home before long." He assured them that he had fully recovered from the injuries received in the crash except for his back which "ached a little yet." Harry Denison landed back in Canada on August 5, 1945. His postcard arrived in October.

Now I had clearly established that Denison was not the murder victim. However, one undeniable fact remained: a young Canadian had been murdered in Frankenberg after he was taken prisoner following the raid on Chemnitz on March 5/6, 1945. Who was he? I had to go back to the drawing board.

CHAPTER 4

Back to the Drawing Board

The report of the Canadian War Crimes Investigation Unit about the murder in Frankenberg had mentioned the names of one witness, Alfred Hermann Paul, and a possible witness, a Dr Katz or Kaatz. My attempts to find any information about Paul or Ka(a)tz in or near Leipzig were unsuccessful. However, from Dr Ahnert's account of "Denison's" murder, I had the names and addresses of three eyewitnesses who, in 2000, had told Eberhard Hübsch that they had seen a young Canadian airman beaten to death in a street in Frankenberg. Through my cousin Fritz Neidhardt, who lives in Chemnitz, I obtained the telephone numbers of those three witnesses. I telephoned each of them and introduced myself. I explained that I was investigating the murder they had witnessed at the end of World War II. All three were very cooperative.

The first witness I called was Anneliese (Anni) Bodenschatz, who is still living in Frankenberg. Speaking German with the soft Saxon accent still very familiar to me, she told me that her apartment is just around the corner from where she saw the murder. Her home is also just a few blocks from where I lived as a 13-year-old in 1945.

In the article Dr Ahnert wrote in 2001, he recorded what Frau Bodenschatz had told Eberhard Hübsch during a brief telephone conversation a year earlier. Frau Bodenschatz's account can be summarized as follows:

> I was walking uphill on Äussere Freiberger Strasse [then called Hindenburgstrasse] when I heard a commotion. I saw German soldiers escorting a tall, strapping, good-looking young man, coming downhill from the [army] barracks ... walking toward centre town. From that direction, four men were coming, armed with wooden clubs. Just in front of the Werner & Dittrich sawmill, they chased the Canadian from one side of the street to the other, beating him until he was dead.

Ahnert had recorded that Frau Bodenschatz thought the Canadian airman had died of his injuries later that day in the hospital. And he added something else that I found puzzling:

> Frau Bodenschatz remembered that the prisoner had a maple leaf symbol on his uniform, which identified him as a Canadian.

A maple leaf? It was easy to establish that RCAF airmen did not have any maple leaf insignia on their uniform in 1945. Furthermore, I doubted whether anyone in Germany at that time would have made the connection between a maple leaf symbol and Canada.

Hoping to clear up the inconsistencies in the story, I asked Frau Bodenschatz to tell me everything she remembered. At first, she said that she couldn't add very much to what she had already told Hübsch, but she was happy to discuss the case with me. She more or less reiterated what I had already learned from reading Ahnert's typescript.

When I questioned her about the maple leaf, she admitted that she didn't really remember that particular detail and that she had probably heard about the maple leaf connection much later.

"How did you know that the victim was Canadian?"

"I can't recall."

I also asked her about the other discrepancy reported by Ahnert. "Did you see the man die in the street, or did he die at the hospital?"

"I don't know. I had heard that he died at the hospital."

"Which hospital? The town hospital or the military hospital at the barracks?"

"I don't know."

"So you didn't actually see whether he was dead immediately after the beating?"

"It is possible, but I don't remember."

Otherwise, her recall seemed to be good. Unfortunately, Frau Bodenschatz said she could not remember the exact date of the murder. When I asked her about the possible perpetrators, she mentioned "the group around Max Florschütz." She said that she had given that information to Hübsch when he interviewed her over the telephone.

I told her I would be in Germany in May, and made arrangements to meet her. She cautioned me again:

"I don't know whether I have anything to add. It was such a long time ago. Also, I didn't really see the actual beating close up, you know. I heard something after I had passed the prisoner and the soldier. Then, when I heard a loud commotion, I looked over my shoulder and saw the man lying there on the other side of the street. I know he had dark hair."

The next witness I telephoned was Ulrich Köhler, who now lives in Noschkowitz, a small village about 30 kilometres north of Frankenberg. As a retired agricultural official, he is still very active and keeps horses as a hobby. He was 15 years old in March 1945. This is a summary of his account as reported by Ahnert:

The Allied air attack against Chemnitz took place on March 5, 1945. One of the attacking planes must have been hit by German anti-aircraft fire. It crashed in the vicinity of Rossau [a village about 15 kilometres north of Frankenberg]. The airman was able to save his life by bailing out. He became a prisoner of war and was taken to the barracks in Frankenberg.

I was 15 at the time. I lived with my parents in a house on the street that is now called Äussere Freiberger Strasse. Since there was no school, I was home and bored. I often looked out the window into the street where there was always something going on. From our kitchen windows, I could look uphill and downhill as far as the railway crossing. The Werner & Dittrich sawmill was across the street from us.

One morning — I can't exactly recall the date — I was looking out the window again when I saw something unusual. A German soldier with rifle and steel helmet came walking down the hill. He was escorting a man wearing a non-German uniform. Both of them were walking on the right side of the street, directly next to the sidewalk. When they had come to the corner of Amalienstrasse, suddenly three men rushed from behind the fence and beat the prisoner with clubs until he fell to the ground. (I thought I recognized one of them as an SS man from our neighbourhood.) The victim could still move to the other side of the street, where he remained lying on the sidewalk in front of Naumann's house. The blood stains were still there the next day. One or two pedestrians walked by without getting involved because the soldier was standing right there.

A young man ran uphill, probably to the barracks. Soon, a truck arrived, and the lifeless body was taken away. We heard later that the victim had been a Canadian, probably one of the downed airmen.

I described the scene to my mother, who had not been in the room. We both came to the conclusion that this crime must have been planned. It was probably meant as revenge for the air raid.

When I spoke with Ulrich Köhler on the telephone, he confirmed that what he remembered was essentially what Ahnert had recorded. He was surprised when I told him that the identity of the Canadian was unknown. He, too, had assumed that Hübsch and Miedtank had named the right man. Köhler was very interested in the case and promised to help. We agreed to meet during my trip to Germany in May. I was still wondering why the Canadian War Crimes Investigation Unit had said "early April" instead of "early March." I asked Köhler whether he remembered the exact date of the murder, but he was not absolutely certain. He said it could have been the day after the major attack of March 5/6, or perhaps a few days later.

Shortly after my telephone conversation with Köhler, he called me back. He said that he had looked up some of his old records. He could now confirm that he had left Frankenberg on April 6, 1945, when he was sent to the town of Bautzen in eastern Saxony, close to the front. There, the 15-year-old served in the Volkssturm, the hastily established German home defence formation cobbled together from men up to 60 and boys 15 and older who weren't already serving in the regular armed forces. The crime certainly couldn't have been committed after April 6, 1945, because Köhler couldn't have witnessed it any later than on that date. This narrowed the time frame somewhat.

Ahnert had speculated that the SS man whom Ulrich Köhler had seen might have been Hans Hunger, who had belonged to a small group in Frankenberg that established a Nazi party cell as early as 1924. As the source for this assumption, he refers to Max Kästner.

Max Eduard Reinhold Kästner (1874–1959) was a teacher, local historian, and naturalist. In 1938, on the occasion of Frankenberg's 750th anniversary, he edited a book about the town called *Aus dem Leben einer kleinen Stadt* (From the Life of a Small Town). In the chapter "Frankenberg in Adolf Hitler's Reich — Frankenberg Before and After the Rise of National Socialism," Hans Hunger is mentioned as one of several early Party members, "a small cadre of active warriors who carried the ideas of the Führer in their hearts, disseminated them and thus contributed to the victory of these ideas."

Speculating further about the perpetrators of the murder, Ahnert also discussed Max Florschütz, mentioned by Frau Bodenschatz:

> I know that the leader of the group is said to have been Max Florschütz, janitor at the high school (opposite the elementary school). According to the local history … by Max Kästner (p. 312), Florschütz was an NSDAP [Nazi Party] town councillor, who had been a Nazi activist as far back as 1932.

When Ahnert was investigating the murder of the Canadian airman in 2001, he learned at the Frankenberg archives that the cemetery administrator in 1945 had been Lydia Birkner. She had died, but Ahnert was able to contact her son, Dr Siegfried Birkner, in Berlin. In March 1945, Birkner had been away as a soldier, but when he returned to Frankenberg, his mother told him that "a group around Florschütz" had murdered a Canadian airman who was buried at the cemetery. Birkner himself had seen the grave to which the body had been moved in June 1945.

In his typescript, Dr Ahnert noted that the present administrator of the cemetery in Frankenberg, Frau Schleicher, knew that the body of an unknown Canadian airman had been buried in a certain area of the cemetery. Ahnert had gone over some of the cemetery records already. In his paper, he reported that the airman's body was exhumed on June 1, 1945, and laid to rest again in a different grave, in Section B, Plot B 4, very close to the main entrance of the cemetery.

Ahnert seems to have been frustrated about his inability to find more information. He wrote: "Why are there no records of the Canadian airman's name, date of birth, date of death and date of burial? Unless hitherto unknown documents regarding this event are located, it will remain a grey zone about which we can only speculate."

It was precisely that "grey zone" I was hoping to penetrate. I tended to agree with Ahnert's conclusion: "It is unlikely that the Canadian had no ID papers on him when he was taken prisoner." Ahnert continued:

This murder of a prisoner of war was clearly a violation of the 1907 Hague Convention on the treatment of POWs, and the perpetrators [knew that they] could be brought to trial by the victors after the war ... he had to be buried without a trace. His identification documents were destroyed. He was interred anonymously in a cloak and dagger operation without entry in the cemetery records, probably among the graves at the lower end of the cemetery where prisoners of war, forced labourers, etc. were buried.

Ahnert noted that an oak cross was erected over the grave with the inscription, "*Hier ruht ein unbekannter kanadischer Soldat, der noch in der Kriegsgefangenschaft sein Leben lassen musste*" (Here rests an unknown Canadian soldier, who had to lose his life while still a prisoner of war). He was unable to learn who had ordered the re-burial or who was responsible for erecting the oak cross. Of course, the grave and the cross no longer existed because as Ahnert discovered, the "unknown airman" had been exhumed once again on December 8, 1948, and moved by an unknown authority to an unknown location.

I telephoned Frau Schleicher, cemetery administrator in Frankenberg. Yes, she had heard of the case. No, she had no records from that period. She informed me that all the old cemetery records had been turned over to the *Stadtarchiv* (town archives). I contacted the archivist, Marion Rau, and told her what I knew of the case. She remembered that Dr Ahnert had already searched the cemetery records without finding much. Nevertheless, I made an appointment to see her in mid-May. She promised to make all relevant records available to me.

I also telephoned the third witness, Lieselotte Braune, who is still living in Frankenberg. She was born in 1927. In 1945, as a young woman, she was doing compulsory service as a clerk at the Military Registration Office in the Frankenberg barracks.[1] Here is a summary of her memories of the events, based on Hübsch's interview, reported by Ahnert:

> I remember being sent home from work early, before noon. My co-worker [Christa Böhme] and I were walking downhill on Äussere Freiberger Strasse, on the sidewalk. Suddenly, close to the curb in front of Naumann's villa, we saw a lifeless human body, covered in blood. His head was facing down-hill, toward the town. We walked directly past the body without stopping. We could see no sign of life. I remember that the street was almost deserted.

Frau Braune told me that Christa Böhme, the woman who accompanied her, can no longer be traced, since she left Franken-berg for West Germany a long time ago. Frau Braune agreed to meet me during my trip to Germany, but warned that she couldn't add anything to what she had already told Hübsch. Neither could she exactly pin down the date, although she thought it was soon after the big attack on Chemnitz.

During one of my many telephone conversations with Dr Koch at that time, he mentioned that Uwe Fiedler, Director of the Schlossbergmuseum in Chemnitz, was writing his doctoral dis-sertation on the bombing of Chemnitz. I planned to spend some of my time in Germany in Chemnitz, and thought that Fiedler might be able to provide me with more information about what happened that night in 1945. I called him and found him most cooperative. I was looking forward to meeting him.

I also contacted the largest newspaper published in the Chemnitz area, the *Freie Presse*. I spoke with Andreas Luksch, the editor responsible for the Frankenberg region. I filled him in on the story, which he found fascinating. I faxed him the basic background information. In an article he described why I was coming to Germany and asked readers who might know anything about the case to come forward.

I made plans to fly to Germany. My private investigation was by now not only time-consuming, it was also becoming expensive. I booked my flight to Frankfurt, arranged for a rental car, and worked out an itinerary for all my appointments.

Reading the accounts of the eyewitnesses and talking with them and the other sources on the telephone had not added very much material to my investigation. I knew how the airman was murdered. I had some clues who some of the perpetrators might have been. But I still had no idea who the victim was. Most of the jigsaw puzzle's pieces were still missing. I was looking forward to being in Frankenberg again, to meeting the witnesses, and in particular to doing some digging in the town archives.

A Process of Elimination

In preparation for my trip to Germany in May 2004 I organized my many notes and established some priorities for further research. To achieve maximum results from my anticipated interviews of the witnesses in Germany and my work at the Frankenberg archives, I needed to have a clear understanding of the many loose threads. Because of my numerous forays to the DND archives and Library and Archives Canada in Ottawa during this period — a round trip of 160 kilometres — I sometimes felt I was living on Highway 417.

I also went back to the Ottawa office of the Commonwealth War Graves Commission (CWGC), where Joanne Neville suggested that their head office in Maidenhead near London might be able to conduct a name search by "cemeteries of origin." We asked Maidenhead to look for the name of Frankenberg in Saxony. A week or so later, I received the following disappointing e-mail from Carol Gamble of the CWGC Enquiries Section in Maidenhead:

Our archive records are not kept by the original cemetery names from where exhumations may have taken place, but only by the current names of the cemeteries. Therefore, it is not possible to carry out a search for previous place of burial without the name of the casualty and thus where they are now buried ... I am sorry I cannot be more helpful in this instance.

Immediately after the war, the four occupying powers (British, American, French, and Soviet) had ordered the German municipal authorities to report all known graves of Allied soldiers and other foreign citizens on German soil. Following up on these reports, British graves registration units travelled around Germany to locate the graves of Commonwealth soldiers. In most cases, the bodies were then exhumed and moved to British or Allied war cemeteries established in Germany. However, in some cases, the bodies were moved to war cemeteries outside Germany (to Belgium, Netherlands, France, Czechoslovakia, and Poland).

As far as the Canadian airman was concerned, I only knew that on December 8, 1948, his body had been moved from Frankenberg. I assumed that the exhumation had been performed by an Allied unit and that the body had been moved to one of the many Allied military cemeteries in Germany. But which one? According to the Commonwealth War Graves Commission there are 44 cemeteries in Germany with Commonwealth war graves. Sixteen of them include the graves of Canadians. In total, these 16 cemeteries hold the remains of 3,226 Canadians.[1]

Where to start? First of all, I thought it would be safe to rule out any cemetery outside Germany. I couldn't imagine any western Allied military authority shipping a Canadian body to Communist Czechoslovakia or Poland in December 1948 — while the Cold War was heating up. I believed that bodies of western Allied soldiers removed from the Soviet Occupation Zone (which became the German Democratic Republic on October 7, 1949) would likely have been taken to Allied cemeteries located in Germany, as close as possible to the original burial place. Berlin was certainly a good guess. Although it lies about 200 kilometres to the north, it is the closest Commonwealth war cemetery to Frankenberg.

Assuming that the "unknown airman's" body had been moved to Berlin, one way I could have proceeded would have been to check the personnel records of all 527 Canadians buried in the 1939–1945 Berlin War Cemetery and of the 15 buried in the Berlin South-Western Cemetery, hoping to find one whose body had been moved there from Frankenberg. Then, if that didn't bear fruit, I could have moved on to the remaining 2,684 Canadian World War II graves in Germany. Before undertaking such an enormous task I wanted to try other lines of investigation.

My next approach was to continue the search by trying to identify the aircraft in which the airman had been a crew member. The most logical conclusion was that it had to be one of the bombers participating in the massive air attack on Chemnitz on March 5/6, 1945. Once again, I turned to Richard Koval's Web site to find out which Canadian bombers from Six Group failed to return from Operation Bluefin (Bomber Command's code name for the March 5/6 bombing of Chemnitz). I also returned to the DND archives in Ottawa to study the handwritten operations report (K Report) for Operation Bluefin.

The report indicated that, in contrast to the operation of February 14/15, this night raid against Chemnitz was very successful. It caused heavy damage to the inner city: "Substantial sections of the city were burned out, and the Siegmar tank engine factory was destroyed." Some crews reported seeing "several large explosions through the cloud." The glow of fires was "visible for 150 miles."[2]

The price paid by the Canadian contingent was high. The very beginning of the operation was already disastrous for Six Group. The 13 participating RCAF bomber squadrons took off in the afternoon of March 5, from seven different bases: 405 (Vancouver), 408 (Goose), and 426 (Thunderbird) from Linton-on-Ouse; 515

(Swordfish) and 432 (Leaside) from East Moor; 419 (Moose) and 428 (Ghost) from Middleton St. George; 424 (Tiger) and 433 (Porcupine) from Skipton-on-Swale; 429 (Bison) from Leeming; 431 (Iroquois) and 434 (Bluenose) from Croft, 420 (Snowy Owl) and 425 (Alouette) from Tholthorpe. The Vancouvers (405 Squadron), which were stationed in Leeming, Bedfordshire, contributed 16 Pathfinders. The only Canadian squadron in Six Group not to take part in the raid was 427 (Lion) stationed at Leeming.

In total, Bomber Command launched 760 Lancaster and Halifax bombers against Chemnitz, of which 40 were lost. More than a quarter of this bomber force (195 aircraft) had come from Six Group, which consisted of RCAF squadrons. Nineteen of the 40 lost aircraft were from Six Group, that is, almost half of all the planes lost in this attack were Canadian. Seven Canadian planes crashed on takeoff in England due to severe icing.

It was still full daylight when the planes took off. Sky conditions had been described as "layers of variable strato-cumulus cloud," with a freezing level at 5,000 feet (1,500 metres), and "thin medium layers between 10,000 and 20,000 feet [3,000 and 6,000 metres] … with a moderate icing index." However, a cloud formation measuring about 15 kilometres in diameter developed between Tholthorpe and Linton. It caused most of the problems. Some staff suspected sabotage, but it was later ruled out, and all the crashes were blamed on freak weather conditions.

At Linton-on-Ouse, three Halifax bombers from the Thunderbird Squadron crashed within minutes after takeoff due to severe icing. One of these crashed in York, killing several civilians on the ground. The Snowy Owls also lost two aircraft immediately after takeoff. Two Halifaxes from Alouette Squadron crashed as well — one near Ousebourne and one near Linton. Thus, 40 Canadian airmen from Six Group died before the course had been set for Chemnitz. In addition, five British civilians were killed and 18 wounded when one of the planes crashed into a school and neighbouring buildings.

Two crashed after a mid-air collision over England. One crashed upon return in England after suffering heavy damage over the target. One ran out of fuel and crashed in England. One was shot down by friendly fire in England. It was piloted by Squadron Leader E.A. Hayes. All crew members died in the crash.

> I was a wireless operator/air gunner with 432 Squadron, East Moor, and was scheduled, with my crew, to go on the Chemnitz operation. Our skipper F/L Johnny Clothier was ordered to go with another crew as second dickey. Our crew stood down and the crew Johnny flew with (Squadron Leader Hayes, pilot) were shot down by friendly fire returning to England. As a result the remainder of my crew had to retrain with a new skipper, F/L Eastman, at 1655 Conversion Unit, Topcliffe. We completed retraining just at war's end. It could be said that our skipper's loss was what saved our lives.[3]

Another Canadian plane crash-landed in England after colliding with one of the crashed aircraft. Thus, 12 Canadian aircraft were lost in England. In addition, one Canadian bomber, a Lancaster piloted by Flying Officer W. Mytruk, encountered severe icing on the return flight from the target and crashed in the Ardennes Mountains in Belgium. Thus, of the 19 Canadian bombers lost, 12 had crashed in England and one in Belgium.

I found a two-page "Report on Aircrew Landing in Allied Occupied Territory," which was based on survivor statements and signed by Flight Lieutenant J.A. Rolfe, "Interrogator for Base Intelligence Officer, No. 64 RCAF Base."

> After having bombed the target on time at 2154 hrs. and on the homeward route, the route and tactics were being followed. This called for a let-down to between 2,000 and 4,000 feet and the A/C [aircraft] was in cloud from 10,000 feet and looking for a break at briefed height.

Icing was encountered and the mid-upper gunner [M/U/G] turret was heavily iced. The M/U/G heard the Pilot say he could not see out because of icing. The Pilot asked the R/G [rear gunner] if he could see any lights below. The R/G replied that he could, and said the lights were a little way below the A/C and made a mental note that they were between 200 and 300 feet below.

The two gunners heard the Navigator tell the Pilot to try and gain height because of being over high ground. By the feeling of the A/C the Pilot endeavoured to climb and had just said "I can't" when the crash occurred ...

The A/C crashed into small spruce trees and caught fire up forward before coming to a standstill. It was snowing in the Ardennes Mountains where the crash occurred at 2345 hrs ... the height of the ground was 2,100 feet.[4]

The flight engineer, Sergeant C.R. Hazelby, was killed instantly. The navigator, Flying Officer W.R. Ashdown, and the bomb aimer, Flying Officer D.A. Wade, died en route to a hospital. The pilot was thrown clear of the aircraft and was taken to the hospital in Liege by members of an RAF regiment stationed at a nearby radar site; he survived his injuries. Three crew members were uninjured in the crash and provided the information for the report: the wireless operator, Pilot Officer Robert Jack Snell; the mid-upper gunner, Flight Sergeant Louis Joseph Chevrier; and the rear gunner, Flight Sergeant Edward L. Scofield.

In addition to the bombers, at least 16 RCAF Pathfinder aircraft from 405 (Vancouver) Squadron were supplied. These planes were stationed at Leeming (then Gransdon Lodge) in Bedfordshire. They were part of Pathfinder Force (PFF). Their task was to mark and illuminate the target area by dropping so-called "Christmas tree" flares. They also dropped "Window," millions of simple aluminum foil strips which appeared as bomber-sized blips on the German radar screens, neutralizing interception by night fighters and flak. There were no reports of any missing Pathfinders after the attack on Chemnitz.

As a result of the Bomber Command attack against Chemnitz on March 5/6, 1945, 90 Canadian airmen were killed or presumed dead. Of these, 79 were from the Canadian squadrons in Six Group, and the others had been flying with squadrons in other groups. Thirty Canadians were taken prisoner of war (26 from Six Group and four from others).

Bomber Command, and in particular the Canadian group, had suffered heavy losses. In fact, Six Group's loss of aircraft and men in this raid was one of the heaviest blows ever suffered by a single group in a single night. On the other hand, the Chemnitz raid was not as disastrous as the raid on Nuremberg on March 30/31, 1944, when Bomber Command lost 106 aircraft and suffered damage to 71 others. Of the 545 airmen who died in the Nuremberg raid, 112 were Canadians. While the Chemnitz raid essentially destroyed the entire inner city in a firestorm, the failed Nuremberg raid "only" damaged 256 buildings.[5] It would take another raid on January 2, 1945, to cause the virtual annihilation of the ancient city by firestorm. Fifty percent of all buildings, including 61,200 homes, not to mention priceless works of Medieval and Renaissance art and architecture, were destroyed.[6]

The hazards of the trip to Chemnitz — including fighters, flak, mid-air collisions and bad weather — were vividly described by RCAF Flight Lieutenant Blyth of 408 (Goose) Squadron:

On our return our base was fogged in, and we were diverted to Mildenhall in Suffolk, east of our airfield. It had been a long trip — 9 hours and 18 minutes, with 6 hours and 30 minutes entirely on instruments. Our fuel gauges read empty when we were given permission to land, but Doug Grey, our engineer, assured me he had calculated the petrol and we were still OK ... As we made our last cross-wind leg, the starboard outer engine started to sputter. Immediately I feathered up the prop, which takes it out of action … Four-engine Halifax bombers do not glide to landing if they run out of fuel: they drop out of the sky like broken elevators in the Empire State Building … My landing was better than expected. When the ground crew refueled us the next day, one member told us we had "a couple of cups of petrol left." That was too close for comfort.[7]

I had now approached my quest for the truth from various angles. Neither the German reports nor the eyewitnesses nor the Canadian war crimes report nor any other archival sources or Web sites had led me to the discovery of the airman's identity. I tried hard to understand the cryptic handwritten Bluefin Interpretations, the Bomber Command Interpretations done immediately after the return of the bombers to their bases.[8] Some of the scribbled figures had been changed (crossed out and/or overwritten). They showed the number of Halifax and Lancaster bombers each squadron had "offered," how many were missing and how many crashed.

It was certainly not easy to evaluate all the different sources to arrive at an overview of RCAF losses in connection with the raid on Chemnitz. No neat accounting was readily available. I had to compile the information laboriously from all these sources, which in some cases contradicted each other. My best source was Richard Koval's Web site. It had information about the March 5/6, 1945, operation against Chemnitz that showed all aircraft (by type, number, and code) from Six Group that took part and were either lost or damaged or had to abort the mission due to malfunction or bad weather. It also showed the rank and name of every crew member.

I calculated that in addition to those aircraft from Six Group that crashed on takeoff and landing, six Canadian bombers were lost over Germany that night.

The six aircraft from Six Group lost over
Germany on March 5/6, 1945

No.	Aircraft	Consequences for crew as listed
1	Halifax III *NA-204*, coded *6U-J* (piloted by F/Lt W. Mitchell)	All eight crew members POW.
2	Halifax III *NP-959*, coded *PT-N* (piloted by F/Lt V. Glover)	Seven crew members POW, one killed.
3	Halifax III *PN-173*, coded *KW-Q* (piloted by F/O J. Desbien)	Four crew members POW, three killed.
4	Halifax VII *NP-799*, coded *OW-J* (piloted by F/Lt Jack Kirkpatrick)	One crew member POW (W.H. Denison), six killed.
5	Lancaster X *KB-858*, coded *SE-G* (piloted by F/O S. Reid)	All seven crew members killed.
6	Lancaster I *NG-458*, coded *QB-H* (piloted by F/Lt D. Ross)	One crew member POW, six killed.

Assuming that the murder victim belonged to a Six Group bomber crew that flew that night, he had to be from one of these six planes. There were 44 crew members on those six aircraft. The records indicated that 21 were taken prisoner and 23 were killed. The crew members shown as killed include those who were

Six of a seven-man Canadian Bomber crew.

originally reported missing/presumed dead. The murder victim
could have been any one of these 44 men.

Of course, I ruled out number four on my list, the Halifax VII
from 426 (Thunderbird) Squadron, piloted by Flight Lieutenant
Jack Kirkpatrick. The murdered airman could not have belonged
to its crew because I knew that all had been killed in the crash —
in the distant Harz Mountains — except for Harry Denison who,
contrary to German sources, had returned to Canada safely.

At the beginning of my investigation, I had assumed that all
surviving crew members of a bomber would land in the same
narrow area, near the crash site. It never occurred to me that the
murder victim might have belonged to a plane whose crew was
widely scattered while parachuting to safety. For that reason, I
had found Denison, the "sole survivor" of Halifax VII *NP-799*,
such a likely victim, just as Miedtank and Hübsch had. The sole
survivor of Lancaster I *NG-458*, number six on my list, Flight
Sergeant C. Antonek, struck me as another likely case. Then I
thought of the opposite: was it likely that the victim was the sole
casualty from a plane whose other crew members all survived?

That lead me to consider Pilot Officer J. Kastner from plane number two, Halifax III *NP-959*, as another good possibility.

Based on these initial assumptions, I set aside number one, Mitchell's Halifax III from 415 (Swordfish) Squadron, because its whole crew had survived. And I also decided, at least for the time being, to disregard number five, Reid's Lancaster X *KB-858* from 431 (Iroquois) Squadron, because all its crew members were reported killed in the crash, and at the time I thought a survivor would have to be listed. (Later, I learned that this bomber had been attacked by a Luftwaffe night fighter, and crashed with its full load still on board, near Oberweidbach, in the state of Hesse, long before it had come anywhere near Chemnitz.)

So initially, my search was now down to three planes, number two (piloted by V. Glover), number three (piloted by J. Desbien), and number six (piloted by D. Ross). Time was running short. I would soon have to leave for Germany. Just before my departure, I decided to investigate the two aircraft that seemed most likely. At Library and Archives Canada in Ottawa, I ordered the personnel files of Kastner, the only crew member listed as killed in aircraft number two, and of the crew members who were killed in aircraft number six (where only Antonek survived).

Kastner's plane, from 420 (Snowy Owl) Squadron, bombed the target as scheduled and was on its return flight from Chemnitz.[9] It crashed near Bad Kreuznach, which is west of the Rhine, hundreds of kilometres west of Chemnitz and Frankenberg. Kastner had died "within hours of being taken prisoner in a German hospital," and he was eventually buried at the war cemetery in Choloy, France. He could not have been the Frankenberg murder victim. I therefore struck this aircraft off my list.

Next, I considered the crash of aircraft number six on my list, the Lancaster I *NG-458* of 424 (Tiger) Squadron. Again, a sole survivor was listed (who was taken prisoner of war): Flight Sergeant C. Antonek. For a day or so, I speculated that Antonek might have been the victim. But since his personnel file was not available at the archives, I knew with virtual certainty that he did not die in the war. From Richard Koval's Web site I knew the names of the other six crew members: Ross, Rayner, Weaver, Cash, Seaby, and Atchison. They were all listed as killed. Sergeant Rayner was an RAF airman flying in a Canadian plane, so his file would not be at the archives. From the remaining five personnel files I learned that Flight Sergeant Antonek had been repatriated to Canada after he was released from a POW camp. I struck him off my list.

But I also learned that this plane had crashed not too far from Frankenberg. For that reason alone, I immediately suspected that the murder victim might have been among this crew. My suspicion and excitement grew when I realized from the documents that some of the crew members listed as dead had originally been reported as "missing and presumed dead." I investigated their files further.

All five personnel files contained copies of Flight Sergeant Antonek's debriefing report, which he had given after his return to England from the POW camp. From this report I learned the following. Just before their RCAF Lancaster bomber had reached the target, it collided with "one of our fighter aircraft."[10] Antonek was able to bail out, but he couldn't say whether anyone else got out before the plane crashed. The Lancaster came down near Königshain. After being taken prisoner, Antonek had helped his German captors to identify the remains of his crew mates. However, only two bodies could be identified, those of Pilot Officer J. Atchison and Flying Officer F. Seaby. These were later buried in the cemetery of nearby Altmittweida. The villages of Königshain and Altmittweida are only about 20 kilometres north of Frankenberg and very close to Rossau, which had been named as a possible crash site by eyewitness Ulrich Köhler.

In addition to the bodies of Atchison and Seaby, Antonek and the Germans found "body parts strewn all over the crash site." Antonek was unable to identify anyone from these gruesome remains. However, the Germans showed him two unopened parachutes. One of these belonged to one of the two crew members who could be identified. The other belonged to Weaver, and it was therefore concluded that Weaver must have died as well.

From this information, or rather from the lack of more information, I speculated that another crew member might have survived the crash. One of the "missing and presumed dead" could have successfully bailed out of the plane (as Antonek did), or walked away from the wreck, to be captured later and held prisoner in Frankenberg. It was a fairly unlikely scenario, but I couldn't rule it out. In Flying Officer Cash's file,[11] I located a document which stated that a French prisoner of war had found Cash's ID card "near the wreckage of a bomber" which he said had collided with a fighter escort. With that information, it now seemed likely to me that Cash, too, had died in the crash.

This left the pilot, Flight Lieutenant Donald Alexander Ross, as the most likely candidate. His personnel file seemed to confirm my suspicion.[12] Bomber Command had reached the official verdict that Ross was missing: "Presumably died in crash, but no identified remains."

Cash, Rayner, Ross, and Weaver are all commemorated at the Runnymeade Memorial as airmen who died without a known grave. Nevertheless, based on the contents of these files at the Library and Archives of Canada, Ross was still my most likely candidate. However, I couldn't follow up this lead or do more research because it was time to leave for Germany. On the flight across the Atlantic, I summarized the rather meagre results of my investigation to date: Denison was not the murder victim; Ross could be the murder victim. I was pinning all my hopes on the archival material I might find in Frankenberg.

CHAPTER 6

Target Chemnitz

The main goal of my trip to Germany in May 2004 was, of course, to discover the identity and possibly find the grave of the "unknown Canadian airman." I also wanted to visit and photograph the murder site in Frankenberg, meet and talk with the eyewitnesses, and photograph them. And I was interested in learning more about the bombing of Chemnitz. I had an appointment to see museum director Uwe Fiedler in Chemnitz and archivist Marion Rau in Frankenberg. I was also hoping that some people had responded to the article in the *Freie Presse* and contributed new information or insights.

I flew to Frankfurt and first did some visiting, taking the train to get around in the "old states" (the former West Germany). In Cologne, I rented a car and drove east to Chemnitz, my hometown. There, I stayed with my cousin Fritz Neidhardt. Fritz had been a textile engineer. After reunification in 1990, Saxony's textile mills were dismantled. The entire industry was dead. In his mid-fifties, Fritz was unable to find any other gainful employment in the depressed "new states" (the former East Germany). With time on his hands and a natural talent as a sleuth, he had done marvellous work as a genealogical detective for me in the past. He now generously offered his help with my current project.

On May 19, Fritz and I met with Uwe Fiedler, the dynamic and enthusiastic director of the Schlossbergmuseum in Chemnitz. The museum, which occupies part of a restored twelfth-century building complex, is dedicated to the history of the city. In 1995, to commemorate the 50th anniversary of the major air attack that had destroyed most of the city, the museum presented a major exhibition called "Target Chemnitz." The exhibition documented not only the destruction of Chemnitz, but also the political and military events leading to the carpet bombing of civilian populations, first by the Luftwaffe in Poland, the Netherlands, and England, then — on a vastly greater scale — by the Allies against every major German city.[1] The museum's exhibition, its publications, and its director all emphasize the fact that the indiscriminate bombing of civilian populations was an outcome of wartime escalation and not something the Allies had suddenly invented toward the end of World War II.

After the meeting with Uwe Fiedler, he invited us to tour the museum, which covers the history of Chemnitz from prehistoric times to the present. Although we were running out of time, I had a close look at some photos of my hometown after the firestorm. I remembered that time only too well:

March 5/6, 1945

The first air-raid alert came at nine in the evening of Monday, March 5, 1945. We were in Frankenberg, only 15 kilometres from Chemnitz. The sirens wailed all over town. Near the end of the war, not only the large cities, but many small towns and even villages in Germany were severely bombed. We always expected the worst. But in this case, Chemnitz turned out to be the prime target. We all listened to the wire broadcast message to find out whether we should go to the basement shelter. Suddenly, I heard strange rustling noises outside. When I opened one of the blackout curtains just a crack to look out, I saw that the night had been turned into day. What seemed like hundreds of aerial flare bombs (commonly known as Christmas trees) had been dropped, preparing the target for the attack. We ran down to the cellar. I was still in the stairway when all hell broke loose. The world seemed to be coming to an end. My ears burst from the thunder and roar, the crashing and howling of bombs and aerial mines. No, we were not being attacked. It was distant Chemnitz. Yet the house shook as in an earthquake.

What about our relatives in the city? My grandmother, my two aunts, my five young cousins? Could they possibly survive this inferno? By 10 p.m., the sirens in Frankenberg sounded the all-clear, a long, even wail without undulations. It was all over. We ran outside. Tears came to my eyes. In spite of the cloud cover and the falling snow, we saw that the western sky was a bright, solid sheet of flame. The city was on fire. There were no communications now. No telephone, no radio, no wire broadcast. Miraculously, the power was still on in our town.

Another alert was sounded at midnight when the second attack began. The sounds we heard were even more horrifying than the first. The third raid followed at 4 a.m. I have no recollection of what anyone said or did during those long hours. Did we just sit in the basement? Did we cry and hope? Did we stand in the street and stare or go back to bed? It was still dark and the snow was still falling when, early in the morning, my mother, my aunt, and I took our two four-wheel handcarts. We walked to the highway and toward the burning Chemnitz. A steady stream of destitute, blackened, bleeding, limping, and bandaged people — almost all women and children — was pouring out of the dead city toward Frankenberg and — I suppose — in all other directions as well. With carts and baby carriages, knapsacks and suitcases, and bundles of bedding, they were all fleeing from hell. It was a miserable trek of humanity.

We asked people: "Have you heard about the Kassberg?" It was the part of town where one of my aunts was living with her three children.

"It's a sea of flames."

"What about Furth?" That's where my grandmother, another aunt, and her children had moved after they had been bombed out before.

"Oh, Furth is one of the worst-hit areas, and the inner city is completely gutted, wiped out."

But someone else said that some houses were still standing in my grandmother's neighbourhood. We didn't meet any of my relatives. Later that morning, as we kept walking on the highway, there was another air attack on the city. Finally we met one of my aunts. She was holding two of my little cousins by the hand, while their teenage maid was pushing the baby carriage with the youngest in it. Their faces were blackened from soot. Their clothes were thickly covered with snow. They were all in a complete state of shock. Their home was in a five-storey apartment building. A bomb had hit the sidewalk right in front of the house, leaving a huge crater. An air mine had come down in the back yard. Everything was chaos. Some walls had collapsed, all the windows were broken, ceilings were down, the roof was gone. The family had been in the basement shelter. They were all alive. My mother and my aunt walked back to Frankenberg with them. I was told to keep walking toward Chemnitz until I found the other relatives.

About noon, farther along the road, I met my "Berlin" aunt with my two other young cousins. After they had been bombed out in Berlin, they had come to Chemnitz to live with my grandmother. Then, on Tuesday, February 6, my grandmother's house, a duplex in a quiet residential street with lots of gardens, was destroyed in an attack by the 8th U.S. Army Air Force. A bomb had hit a corner of the house and turned the front yard into a huge crater. The second storey of the house had collapsed above them like a matchbox. However, the whole roof and attic structure had come to rest on my grandmother's huge, solid-oak wardrobe. The cellar stairway was gone. Half the cellar was filled with rubble — including the air-raid shelter. They all survived the collapse of the house, but soon they noticed a smell of gas. The gas line had ruptured, and gas was escaping into the cellar. They were able to dig themselves out. They spent the rest of the attack in the undamaged house next door. There, they found a temporary refuge in one room for about a month.

During the night of March 5, the house where my grandmother, aunt, and cousins were staying was hit as well. My grandmother was now bombed out for the second time, my aunt and her family for the third time. They had lost even the few things they had saved the other times. They all went into a crowded air-raid bunker. When I met my aunt on the road, she was terribly upset because she didn't know where Grandmother was.

"That crazy woman left early this morning. Said she would walk to work! There was no stopping her. She walked right into the burning city after we were bombed out."

I sent the "Berlin" family on their way to Frankenberg and continued walking along the road to Chemnitz. I passed hundreds of people. I had almost given up on my dear grandmother. At last, late in the afternoon, as the sun came out behind the clouds and shone directly into my eyes, I spotted her staggering along the road. She was injured and bandaged. She told me what had happened. In the morning, as soon as she arrived in the large paved yard of the only partly damaged complex of buildings where she worked as a cook, the daytime raid on Chemnitz began. It had come without warning because all the air-raid sirens had been silenced by the night attack. Suddenly, she saw a fighter plane swoop down low, coming straight at her. It fired at her as she was running across the yard seeking shelter in one of the buildings. Machine gun bullets sprayed the pavement right next to her. She managed to escape unharmed. When she realized that she was the only person who had reported for work, she made her way through streets of burning rubble, often stepping over corpses, to the Kassberg area to find her other daughter and grandchildren. When she finally arrived at my aunt's house on Hübschmannstrasse, they were just preparing to leave. As my grandmother helped them to gather some of their belongings in the ruined apartment, a large window frame came loose, crashed down and hit her in the back. While the others left and walked to Frankenberg, *Oma* stayed in the city to find a place where she could be bandaged. She was afraid of bleeding to death. Now she was glad to see me. I hugged her, but she cried in pain when I touched her back. We walked together. It was dark by the time we arrived in Frankenberg.

It can be assumed that the vast majority of the people on the ground in Chemnitz were civilians: women, children, and men older than military age. There also would have been soldiers in barracks, at administrative centres, and on leave. Other men in uniform would have included members of the SS, Storm Troopers, Hitler Youth, and a large number of Nazi Party functionaries. The Nazi Party and its numerous organizations maintained an overblown bureaucratic apparatus with central, regional, and local offices, from the paramilitary Motorist Corps to the National Socialist Welfare Organization. No aspect of life in Nazi Germany had escaped regulation and political structure. With the end of the war in sight, most of this administrative network had already been severely interrupted through the demolition of transportation and communication lines throughout Germany. Chemnitz itself had already suffered much damage to residential areas and industrial plants, following several Allied bombing raids in 1944 as well as on February 6, 1945, and especially on February 14/15, 1945. Thus, the situation in the city was by no means normal when the major firebombing of March 5/6, 1945, began.

The population had been expecting a massive raid; it would have been unreasonable not to. After all, Magdeburg, Halle, Dresden, and other cities in central Germany had already been devastated in the course of Operation Thunderclap. While the annihilation of Dresden had come as a surprise due to its lack of major industry and to its world-renowned cultural heritage, Chemnitz could claim no such exemption. The city known as the "Saxon Manchester" because of its key role in the German textile industry was also a centre of the auto industry. Another specialty was engineering, the production of machine tools, etc. Anyone approaching Chemnitz from any direction was immediately impressed by its forest of smokestacks. The city was also an important link in the region's railway system. The only reason Chemnitz had not seen any massive bombing raids yet on the scale of Hamburg, Berlin, Cologne, Nuremberg, etc., was its distance from air bases in England.

Chemnitz was a city of factory workers. Most people lived in modest apartments, in walk-up rows of flats that lined the streets. Especially in the less affluent quarters, flats generally did not have bathrooms. A toilet and sink installed on stairway landings were shared by all tenants. As a result of this inconvenience, many families still used chamber pots or commode chairs in their flats, to be emptied in the morning. In the basement was a shared laundry room. Clothes were dried on communal clothes lines in a shared attic. Any washing hung up outdoors would soon be covered in black soot.

Before the war, Hitler had promised to improve social conditions for ordinary workers in Germany. The Nazis had begun to implement some social reforms. Much of their support came from the same "proletariat" that had previously seen Communism as its salvation. However, the war had interrupted programs such as the holiday travel scheme *Kraft durch Freude* (Strength through Joy) and affordable-housing projects. While some new subdivisions with single-family homes surrounded by neat little gardens had sprung up, the vast majority of workers still lived in tenements.

While the inhabitants of Chemnitz were afraid of "the big one," before March 5, they were still hoping to be spared. Many were already speculating that the war might be over before the Allies struck a devastating blow. How much pounding could the German nation still endure? Some had placed their bets on Hitler's much-rumoured "wonder weapon." But when the unmanned, rocket-powered *Vergeltungswaffen* (retaliation weapons), also known as "buzz bombs," caused only moderate damage in Britain instead of turning the tide of the entire war, it became evident to most Germans that it would be only a matter of weeks, at most months, before the final collapse. Certainly very few still believed that the promised *Endsieg* (final victory) was going to be achieved.

The combined 8th U.S. Army Air Force and Bomber Command attacks of March 5/6, 1945, took the lives of 2,105 German civilians in the city of Chemnitz. Considering the severity of the attacks, the large number of heavy bombers, and the enormous amount of explosives and incendiaries dropped during the night and on the following day, it is almost unbelievable that such a relatively small number of people were killed. Probably the main reason civilian casualties were not higher was that every house, every workplace, and every building had a more or less well-constructed *Luftschutzkeller* (air-raid shelter) in the basement. Even before the war started, but especially in the early years of the war, there was an all-out effort to provide every dwelling in Germany with a shelter fortified with steel beams and concrete ceilings and walls. Most shelters were equipped with fireproof doors and survival gear such as water buckets, fire extinguishers, and all kinds of specialized firefighting and rescue implements. In addition, there was a well-organized network of air-raid wardens (mostly women and older men) and runners (mostly Hitler Youth boys and girls). Throughout the war, regularly scheduled air-raid exercises were held, supervised by trained air-raid wardens and their helpers. Every night, from September 1, 1939, to the end of the war, the entire city was blacked out. Should a tiny sliver of light ever shine through carelessly pulled blackout curtains, it would not be long before an angry neighbour would knock on the window and shout: "*Verdunkeln!*" (blackout!) Black tape was pasted over the headlights of cars and trucks, buses and streetcars, leaving only a narrow strip of light to fall onto the pavement. Even flashlights had to be reduced to a pinhole of light. To be seen by others on the dark sidewalks, people wore phosphorescent patches on their shoes or clothing. Since leather was at a premium, many shoes were made with wooden soles. When pedestrians approached, their footsteps could be heard from far away, and that made collisions less likely. In all cities, large public air-raid shelters had been built to accommodate people who were caught by an air raid while away from home. Some of these shelters were so well-constructed that efforts to demolish them after the war failed until heavy charges of explosives were employed.

While nothing had prepared or could prepare Germans for the firestorms caused by massive saturation bombing, the nationwide shelter and rescue system nevertheless saved an untold number of lives that would otherwise have been lost. The reason casualties in Dresden had been so extraordinarily high was that thousands, perhaps a few hundred thousand, of refugees from Germany's eastern provinces were temporarily housed in unsheltered areas of buildings, and — in spite of the season — even in the open. When the March attack came against Chemnitz, the lessons of Dresden had been learned. Relatively few people were left unprotected.

I remember that starting in February, there were air alerts virtually every day. Most of the time we stayed in the cellar, and we didn't dare to venture far from our front door. But gradually we children came to regard this situation as quite normal, and we wondered why the adults were so worried. March 5 proved how right they had been. There was still snow on the ground. The sirens had wailed again, and we were in the cellar. Some of the people living in new houses came to stay with us, hoping that the vaulted masonry in the older houses would resist the bombs better.

Suddenly an air-raid warden came to tell us that "Christmas trees" had been set up. This we had to see. Before the adults could stop us, we older kids went upstairs and outside. What we saw was awesome. The sky was brightly lit, and the so-called Christmas trees very slowly floated down to the ground. We were sent back to the cellar right away because the roar of the bomber formations was coming dangerously close.

And then it began! We were on our knees, a woollen blanket covering our backs and heads. We held our heads down and a clothes pin between the teeth (this was supposed to protect the lungs from the blast). The earth shook. Every hit lifted us off the floor. The cellar wall cracked, and the contents of the sewage tank in the yard poured into the cellar. The stench was horrible. Some older people screamed hysterically and wanted to leave the cellar, saying that the house was hit. But the air-raid warden wouldn't let anyone leave.

I can't say how long this lasted. Suddenly we were told: "Get out! Put out the fire!" We ran into the street: four houses were on fire. People were working the handles of water pumps. We formed bucket chains. One of the homes burned out completely. Another could be saved by the adults who were working feverishly with "water swatters" — rags attached to the handles of shovels which were constantly dipped in water buckets. Soon the pumps were without water. By 3 a.m., a woman whom we hardly knew, came to offer us her bedroom to rest because we were all dead-tired.

In an industrial yard at the edge of our housing development, barrels filled with gasoline exploded, causing chaos. On Sidonienstrasse, people were burned to death in their homes because they had refused to go to an air-raid shelter. I remember that the fires in the ruined houses kept flaring up for days. All the windows in the neighbourhood had been blown out.[2]

Below are a few examples of death notices for victims of the March 5/6 attack. They appeared in the *Chemnitzer Zeitung* (vol. 48, No. 74, April 1/2 — Easter — 1945) under the heading "*Durch Terror gefallen*" (Killed by terror). It can be assumed that no newspapers appeared in Chemnitz immediately after the attack, which destroyed all newspaper facilities. The *Chemnitzer Zeitung* was published on March 12, but no copy can be found. This edition of April 1/2 is the first after the attack included in the microfilm collection in the Chemnitz city archives.

Hildegard Manger, born March 5, 1929. Our dear daughter and sister died on March 5, 1945. In deep sorrow: Kurt Manger and wife, brother Herbert …

Marieluise. It was God's will that on March 5th, we should lose our dear child, age 10. The Alexander Hauptmann family.

Charlotte Eichbichler, née Kühn, born Jan. 27, 1911. My dear wife with her six children were cruelly torn from me on March 5th. In deep sorrow, Max Eichbichler, soldier at the front …

Helene Schmieder, Ursula Schmieder and Alma Schmieder all died on March 5th. It is so painful to have lost my wife, my daughter and my mother all at once. Kurt Schmieder.

This edition of the daily newspaper included 18 death notices for soldiers killed in action and 57 death notices for 127 civilian bombing victims. On the same page, the following public notice appeared:

Mandatory registration of all living quarters
The confiscation of all available living space has been ordered. At the same time, all owners or superintendents of houses, and in their absence the air-raid wardens responsible for them, have been ordered to report immediately how many flats are still inhabitable in their building, or how many can be easily repaired and made habitable again. Detailed information must be given as to the number of rooms, etc. ... Persons failing to comply will be prosecuted ...

An editorial on the front page of the *Chemnitzer Zeitung* of April 3, 1945, entitled "The Horsemen of the Apocalypse" observes that to the surviving citizens of Chemnitz, the four legendary horsemen no longer appear in the form of medieval symbols as depicted by Dürer, Böcklin, and other painters as War, Death, Famine, and Pestilence but

as the heads of Churchill, Stalin, Roosevelt and the "Jews of their court," Baruch, Morgenthau and Ilya Ehrenburg, all wearing the hate-filled countenance of murderers. The modern carriers of death — the bomber squadrons — have risen straight from the underworld ... their breath is poison and fire issues from their nostrils — a devilish pack of horses and riders. Citizens of Chemnitz, stare coldly into their satanic grin and prepare for resistance to the last breath!

Such was the official message in response to Allied strategic bombing, no doubt composed to please Josef Goebbels, the boss of all Nazi journalists. The people's reality took different forms.

The *Freie Presse* of March 6, 1995, quoted 101-year-old Alma Fritzsche, who had been 50 when Chemnitz was attacked by Bomber Command 50 years earlier. She vividly remembered the roar of the bombers in the air and people in the streets running frantically for cover in shelters and in the nearby woods.

Shortly after the raids, I went to the cemetery. I saw people digging mass graves many metres long. They just dumped the bodies in. There were no caskets. Some of the dead were wrapped in blankets, and one had been stuffed inside some kind of cupboard.[3]

Irene Pornitz, née Vogel, was the wife of Ulrich Pornitz, owner of a factory in Chemnitz. In March 1945 she lived on a farm just outside the city. In her diary, she recorded the events of March 5 and 6:

March 5: Horrendous night attack on Chemnitz. The sky blood-red from the burning city. Bombs falling without pause. Five Russians arrive from the factory and report that the whole city has been destroyed, the factory is completely gutted. Uli and I took the sleigh to go into the city. Only got as far as Haydnstrasse. Then everything fire, smoke, collapsing buildings. Mother's house burned out ...

March 5/6: All along Stollberger Strasse, Parkstrasse ... everything burned out, destroyed. Either flames shooting up, or blackened ruins. All that remains of the factory are a few sections of wall. On Stollberger Strasse, thousands of refugees are leaving the city. Black faces, burns, exhausted, apathetic, desperate. They have loaded what's left of their belongings onto handcarts and baby carriages. Little children and old people can't carry on. Some in colourful bathrobes or only wrapped in blankets. An indescribable trek of misery we will never forget. At noon, we walked back, helped people to push and carry. In a ditch, we saw a dead old woman with her blue eyes wide open. Must have died of exhaustion. The night in Chemnitz must have been hell. They say nothing remains of downtown.[4]

No one in Frankenberg was untouched by the catastrophe in Chemnitz either. Yet the town's daily newspaper, the *Tageblatt*, reported nothing at all on March 6. On March 7, it carried two-and-a-half lines on page two, under the heading "The Armed Forces Report of Tuesday." After mentioning the fighting in Slovakia and Pomerania, in East Prussia and on the Lower Rhine (where "English and Canadian troops were driven back from the Xanten area"), a brief laconic passage read:

Last night, Chemnitz was again the target of a heavy attack by the British, who also dropped bombs on cities in the

Downtown Chemnitz a year after the firestorm of March 5/6, 1945.

western, southern and central areas of the Reich. Thirty-two American aircraft, mostly four-engine bombers, were brought down by our anti-aircraft measures.

The same report continued:

In addition to shooting down these British [*sic*] terror bombers, our German aircraft, flying in broad formation over the British Isles, achieved further success by bombing ... industrial and military installations in illuminated towns. London continues to be under retaliation fire.

No mention was made of the devastation caused in Chemnitz, of the firestorm, the heavy civilian casualties, or the crowds of desperate women, children, and old people, many of them suffering from burns and other injuries, who were seeking shelter in Frankenberg.

On March 19, 1945, Bomber Command issued "Interpretation Report No. K. 3899," describing the 8th U.S. Army Air Force attacks on Chemnitz on March 2, 3, and 5 and the Bomber Command attack on March 5. The "general statement," based on reconnaissance photographs taken in the afternoon of March 15, reads as follows:

The hitherto lightly damaged city of Chemnitz has suffered heavily, damage being caused mostly by fire, with about 60% of the fully built-up central area gutted. Heavy damage to suburban areas extends well to the East, North and South. Of the fifty priority industries of the town, seventeen have been damaged. More may have been affected, as all of the industries have not been definitely located.

Chemnitz, the third largest city of Saxony, was an industrial town, famous for its spinning machine manufacture for 80 years, and the home of a large number of Light Engineering

Works, machine tool makers, motor side cars, bicycles, textile products and related industries. It had a peculiar central built-up area, used for commerce, administration and manufacture of small tools, as well as housing a large part of the population in tenements.

The first priority J.E. Reinecke AG, machine tool makers, owning a most important and well equipped plant, were very heavily hit. Almost every building of this large plant was gutted, and some were in addition damaged by high explosives. The Schubert und Salzer AG, at present a small arms manufacturer (Priority 2), also was heavily damaged by fire. Nine Priority 3 plants, manufacturers of a variety of mechanical contrivances, suffered in varying degrees as a result of the attack.

Transportation has been heavily affected. The Priority 2 railway repair shops have about one third of the buildings gutted, the Priority 3 Chemnitz South Goods Depot has every building destroyed by fire, and some tracks cut by craters. The Sonnenberg goods station, the Main Station and the Nikolai Station were all damaged lightly.

The power station and a number of public buildings, including the post office, the court, and the town library, as well as three barracks areas were damaged by fire.

Bomber Command painstakingly calculated the damage caused to various industries, transportation facilities, utilities, and public buildings, and concluded that in addition to 60 percent of the city's "fully built-up area," 29 percent of the less densely developed areas were destroyed or seriously damaged.

Allied bombers attacked Chemnitz again on the evening of Thursday, April 12, 1945.

CHAPTER 7

On the Paper Trail

When I first arrived at my cousin's house in Chemnitz, I was pleased to learn that Fritz had heard from two readers in response to Andreas Luksch's article about my quest. Both happened to live in Sachsenburg, a village just a few kilometres from Frankenberg. As soon as I had unpacked my bags, I telephoned the first, Wolfgang Hammer. He said he would be unable to meet with me since he was leaving shortly on a business trip. However, he told me that his maternal grandfather, Oskar Liebhaber, a Frankenberg police officer, had been assigned to investigate the murder of the Canadian airman in March 1945. He suggested I search in the archives for records of the police investigation. The other respondent was Elfriede Rupprecht, who wrote that she had witnessed the murder. I telephoned her as well, and she agreed to see me. I had high expectations for that meeting.

My appointment with Marion Rau at the Municipal Archives in Frankenberg was for 8:30 a.m. on May 21, 2004. My cousin Fritz and I arrived early, after the short, 20-minute drive from Chemnitz. We had time to look at the house where my mother, my younger sister, and I had lived in 1945. The house in its fresh new coat of plaster looked pleasant and inviting. The garden where I had once buried my treasure no longer existed because another house had been built over it. I wondered whether anyone had found my little box during excavations. The house was just a few blocks from Äussere Freiberger Strasse, then called Hindenburgstrasse, where the murder had taken place. I remembered now what Ulrich Köhler had said in his eyewitness report: "Since there was no school, I was home and bored. I often looked out the window into the street where there was always something going on."

I fully understand what he meant, because my school, too, had been permanently closed by that time. I had also spent much time sitting on a wide window sill with a book, or just looking down into the street, which was called Ludendorffstrasse at the time.[1] Something was always happening in the street: army trucks rolling by belching clouds of black smoke, columns of soldiers marching, horse-drawn supply wagons, officers on horseback, old women pulling rickety handcarts with heavy loads of coal or potato sacks.

Actually, the Frankenberg *Stadtarchiv* (Municipal Archives) was closed that Friday — sandwiched between Ascension Day (a statutory holiday in Saxony) and the weekend. But Frau Rau had kindly agreed to open up on her day off and be available until noon. She had already prepared a number of collections for me to peruse in the research room.

I started by examining some municipal records identified as "Files of the Town of Frankenberg." They included the town's cemetery records. Only some of these dated back to the Nazi era. In February 1944, the *Arbeitsamt* (labour office) in the district capital of Flöha, following an order by the Minister for the Interior, instructed all towns in its jurisdiction to report how many graves of foreign workers and other foreigners they had in their cemeteries. In a letter dated April 4, 1945, the labour office told the Mayor of Frankenberg that there was a discrepancy in numbers: at one time eight graves had been reported, at another time thirteen. The mayor's office was now instructed to provide a complete list including surname, first name, dates of birth and death, and nationality of the deceased. This letter was marked "received" by Frankenberg cemetery administrator Birkner on April 12, 1945.

On April 13, 1945, the acting mayor of Frankenberg told Flöha that there were actually 14 foreigners buried in the town's cemetery. He attached a list of all "civilian labourers and prisoners of war" buried there. The list contained all available information about those buried to date: thirteen civilian labourers, plus an "English" prisoner of war, Matthew Orr (spelled "Mathew"), born September 21, 1915, died January 8, 1945, buried January 12, 1945. I noted that the list did not include an "unknown Canadian." I also saw that the list contained at least one error: one of the labourers was recorded as having died on November 2, 1945, seven months *after* the list was compiled. But this correspondence also illustrates the meticulous care with which the hierarchic Nazi bureaucracy recorded details, even less than a month before the war ended. The fact that neither the death of the Canadian airman murdered in Frankenberg nor the whereabouts of his grave were reported suggests that some officials had deliberately (and illegally) withheld the information.

I found no other wartime records that shed any light on the case I was investigating. The wartime official record of births,

The author examining Frankenberg's wartime cemetery records at the town archives in May 2004.

marriages, and deaths contained no entry indicating the death of a Canadian airman in March or April 1945. However, some of the papers created immediately after the war did.

Still in the cemetery records, under the subject of "Exhumation of bodies and extraordinary events … in 1945," I found a document showing that the town's social welfare office had placed an order worth 50 *reichsmark* with master cabinet maker Jacob for the immediate delivery of a coffin for "1 Canadian, No. 162." The order was stamped June 5, 1945, but it indi-

"Records pertaining to the exhumation of bodies and extraordinary events" at the Frankenberg town archives.

cated that the body was placed in the coffin on June 3, 1945. Evidently the order was issued after the service had already been performed, a practice not uncommon in any bureaucracy. On the order form, the date and place of death as well as the cause of death and the date of burial were left blank.

On Tuesday, June 26, 1945, a public meeting was held in which Mayor Dirks, other town council members, and representatives of Frankenberg's residents took part. Near the bottom of the agenda, under item 19, it was moved by the mayor that "the grave of the Canadian soldier buried at the local cemetery" should be marked by a wooden commemorative cross with "an appropriate inscription." The motion was carried unanimously.[2]

Also in the cemetery records at the town archives, I found a letter written on September 15, 1945, by Dr Wolff, chief medical officer of the former military hospital in Frankenberg, addressed to the *Bürgermeister* (mayor) of Frankenberg.

Before the military hospital is completely closed, I am very concerned that the military hospital cemetery, where the bodies of about 100 soldiers are buried, is brought into a dignified state. The intention is to erect a large oak cross and also to place a commemorative plaque which would contain all the names of the dead and their grave numbers ...

This is necessary particularly because with the improvement of travel, it can be expected that next of kin of the deceased will visit, and the cemetery should therefore be in a dignified state ...[3]

I was unable to find any other documents about the cemetery at the military hospital in the barracks compound. But Dr Wolff's letter proves that there was one in 1945, and that it still held about 100 graves in September 1945. It is quite possible that the murder victim's grave had been there as well, but that the body was moved to the town cemetery in June 1945, to the area where other non-Germans were buried. A likely scenario is that on the day of the crime, a Wehrmacht truck came, picked the body up at the murder site, and took it to the military hospital on the nearby barracks grounds. There, someone in authority decided to bury it secretly at the military hospital cemetery without reporting the death or the burial to the civilian authorities, and without marking the grave with the dead airman's Canadian ID number. There it remained buried until shortly after the war, when, on or about June 1, 1945, it was exhumed and shortly afterwards reburied at the town cemetery, in a marked grave, but still without identification.

I found more post-war correspondence between the District Administration in Flöha and the *Standesbeamte* (registrar of births, marriages, and deaths) in Frankenberg. On November 13, 1945, Flöha asked the registrar to comply with an order by Saxony's chief of police and immediately submit a list of "all citizens of Allied states and other countries" who had died in Frankenberg as prisoners of war, including their name and nationality, time of death, cause of death, place of burial, and condition of grave.

The Frankenberg registrar mailed a list to Flöha, with a covering letter dated the very next day, November 14. The handwritten list included an entry indicating that an "unknown Canadian airman" was reburied in Grave B/4 on June 1, 1945.

Under the heading "Notification of War Dead" I found a report by the *Bestattungsamt* (mortuary office) in Frankenberg, dated April 26, 1946, stating that a "nameless" Canadian airman had been buried the year before at the town cemetery in Frankenberg.

> The grave has been well cared for and is decorated with an oak cross. Buried (reburied) on June 1, 1945. The inscription reads: "Here rests an unknown Canadian soldier who had to lose his life while still a prisoner of war"… Also buried here is an English prisoner of war named Mathew Orr.

On May 2, 1946, the same office requested that the inscription of the cross over the grave be corrected. Apparently, the text had erroneously included the word "American" instead of "Canadian."

> Since the foreign airman buried at the local cemetery (Grave No. B/4, Plot B) is not an American but a Canadian airman, the inscription of the cross erected over his grave must be corrected accordingly.

On June 11, 1946, thirteen months after the end of the war, the town's registrar of births, marriages, and deaths (under *Kriegssterbefall-Anzeigen* [Notification of War Dead]) listed 23 "members of the United Nations" buried in Frankenberg.[4] This list was compiled in compliance with Order No. 163, issued by the Supreme Commander of the Soviet Military Administration to all German municipal authorities in an effort to locate Allied war graves in the Soviet zone of occupation. The list included those already reported in April 1945 (minus the Bulgarian and the Belgian, who had probably been moved to other burial places by this time). It also showed several other "eastern labourers," a few Russians (soldiers?) who had died in Frankenberg shortly after the end of the war, and — as the very last entry — the "nameless Canadian airman, re-buried in Grave No. B/4, Division B, on June 1, 1945."

It is conspicuous that even during that post-war disinterment and reburial in June 1945, his identity was not made known. Neither the date of death nor the original burial site were recorded. Was someone still anxious to keep the identity a secret to prevent a thorough investigation? Was that someone still in an influential or even official position? A handwritten note on the list, obviously entered later, reads: "*am 8.12.1948 überführt*" ("moved on December 8, 1948"). No one had recorded who moved the body or where it was taken. All those important questions remained a mystery. The British soldier, Matthew Orr, was also on this list, with the same mysterious handwritten entry: moved on December 8, 1948.

One of the many notes I made in Frankenberg was a reminder to myself that after my return to Canada, I must ask the Commonwealth War Graves Commission to locate the final resting place of Matthew Orr. He, at least, had a name. I thought, if I can find Orr, I may find the Canadian at the same cemetery.

In summary, the Frankenberg cemetery and death records showed nothing about the death and wartime burial of the Canadian airman. His body was reburied in the town cemetery on June 1, 1945 — three weeks after the war had ended. At some time between that date and April 1946, a wooden cross was erected over his grave. The body was exhumed and moved to an unknown location on December 8, 1948. I had been able to confirm anecdotal reports with documentary evidence, but I was still far from solving the mystery.

I followed up on Wolfgang Hammer's suggestion and searched the few police records available at the archives for references to his grandfather, Oskar Liebhaber. There were some items per-taining to him, but nothing about the murder or its investigation. No daily journals or day-to-day records of police investigations in 1945 were available.

The archivist showed me a stack of index cards with the names and functions of Nazi officials and other Nazi activists in Frankenberg. The cards had probably been prepared by the Antifa, the hastily formed anti-Fascist and pro-Soviet group which briefly administered the area immediately following the war. Until the reunification of Germany, these cards had been stored elsewhere as "restricted material," but the restriction was lifted, and they had just been returned to Frankenberg. I was hop-ing to find the names of Florschütz and Hunger. Both had been named in Ahnert's account as alleged perpetrators of the murder. Florschütz had been a member of the SA, Hunger of the SS. Sur-prisingly, I did not find their names. Had someone removed their cards? If so, who and when?

Later, I received the following fragments of statistical informa-tion from a credible source who does not wish to be identified. Max Florschütz was born in Frankenberg on November 28, 1888. At the time of the murder in 1945, he would have been 56 years old. He was married in the town of Rosswein (Saxony) in 1912. He had four children. I now know exactly where in Frankenberg he lived between 1933 and 1946 and that he was originally a glazier by trade. He then served in the fire brigade where he was promoted to half-platoon leader on April 1, 1934, to master fire-man on July 13, 1936, to senior troop leader on May 19, 1940, and finally to sergeant on June 1, 1943. He was *abgemeldet* (literally "deregistered") two days after the end of the war, on May 10, 1945. It is not clear whether this vague term referred to his dis-missal from the fire brigade or the fact that he left town. He died in Frankenberg on June 10, 1967, at the age of 77.

Certain documents which would have provided more detailed information seem to be no longer in existence. Frau Rau, the archivist, told me that some archival and statistical documents were destroyed during the GDR period. Other municipal records, which might still exist outside the archives, are not readily available. For these reasons, I have been unable to determine the whereabouts of Max Florschütz between 1946 and 1967.

In a letter to the editor of the *Freie Presse*, May 25, 2004, Ernst Rossberg wrote that after Soviet troops occupied Frankenberg, they "arrested SA *Sturmführer* (Lieutenant of the Storm Troopers) Max Florschütz, who has been missing since then ... Rumour had it that he had been linked to the affair about the dead Canadian." The letter writer had been away as a soldier in March 1945. He continued, "When I returned in June 1945, after my brief detention as a POW by the Americans, my father, who personally knew Max Florschütz well, was unable to tell me whether this was correct or not."[5]

This anecdotal information about Florschütz was consistent with what Frau Bodenschatz had already told me, namely that Florschütz had been somehow punished for his alleged crime. However, Rossberg's remark that Florschütz had been "missing since then" is inconsistent with Frau Bodenschatz's statement that she had seen him in town some years after the war, and with the statistical record, which states that he died in Frankenberg in 1962.

I was able to learn even less about Hans Hunger. I obtained the following sketchy details from the same informed source: Between 1933 and 1934, Hans Hunger was listed as an auditor and tax consultant. Later, his profession was recorded as "business manager." Available records only document his residence in Frankenberg during the 1930s, although witnesses confirm that he lived in the town in the 1940s and was definitely there at the end of the war.

I scanned the early March 1945 editions of the town's daily newspaper, the *Tageblatt für Frankenberg und Hainichen*, but found no mention of the murder.

I also read the May 4, 1945, edition of this paper, the last issue before capitulation and the final collapse of the Nazi regime. There I found the following lines, which reminded me of how I felt as we all huddled in the cellar expecting to be killed or tortured when the Red Army reached our town:

> Several villages temporarily occupied by the Soviets have been liberated again. People who had been forced to stay behind have suffered immensely under the Soviet occupation. There are villages where even old women were not spared from rape. One young girl was raped 50 times by the bestial Asiatic hordes and suffered most serious internal injuries.
>
> The things our medical staff have heard in recent days from crying women and girls who had to experience those horrors, are so disgusting that they cannot be reported here …

The Eyewitnesses

Anni Bodenschatz is an active 85-year-old. Her neat senior's apartment on Pestalozzistrasse in Frankenberg is practically around the corner from the scene of the murder. Over a cup of coffee, she reiterated what she had said during our telephone call, but she did give me some more details.

In March 1945 she was a young woman of 25. On a day whose exact date she does not recall, but which she believes was "soon after the big attack on Chemnitz," of March 5/6, 1945, she was walking uphill on Äussere Freiberger Strasse (then called Hindenburgstrasse), accompanied by her sister and two young children (her 3-year-old daughter and her sister's son). On the way the

Eyewitness Anni Bodenschatz of Frankenberg.

group met a soldier escorting a man in a strange-looking uniform, coming from the other direction. She first wondered whether the man might be one of the firemen whose trucks had been parked for a while near the army barracks. This unit of firefighters had come from out of town to help in the rescue efforts in Chemnitz after the firestorm. As the two men came closer, she recognized the younger, uniformed man as a foreign soldier and assumed that he was a prisoner of war. After the two women and the children had passed the two men and had gone a piece farther uphill, they suddenly heard a commotion behind them.

"I looked around and saw that four men were viciously beating the prisoner with wooden clubs. He fell down. Then I saw Hans Hunger coming down the hill, toward the scene of the beating. He seemed disturbed, and his face looked pale and distraught. I remember asking Hunger: Is this in revenge of the attack on Chemnitz? I don't remember Hunger's reply. We kept walking uphill with the children. Soon after this event, there was another air-raid alert, and we had to run to find a shelter. I don't know what happened to the body afterwards."

"Had Hunger been in uniform?" I asked.

"No, he was wearing civilian clothes."

"Was he a member of the SS?"

"No, I don't think so."

"What happened to Hans Hunger?"

"He disappeared after the war. I never heard of him again."

"Why do you think he disappeared?"

"So many people just disappeared at that time. No one asked questions. Maybe they took him away."

"Who?"

"The Russians. Or maybe he just left."

Later I was to hear more about Hans Hunger from another witness, Dr Ewald Kuschka of Flöha, who came forward as a result of a third newspaper article about my investigation and who took a different view. Kuschka is about my age, and was a student in the same high school I attended in 1945, although I don't recall knowing him then. He first wrote a letter to the editor and then sent me a copy of his typewritten memoirs. There, on page 87, he writes:

> In the afternoon of March 6 [1945], something terrible happened on Hochwartenberg: Just below the Figura Kubik villa, I saw a large pool of blood in the street. A lot of shocked people were standing around ... From what the people said, I gradually learned what had happened.

Kuschka recalls that the people were outraged about the attack against a prisoner of war. These people said that the Canadian victim had been a very young man, and that the German guard had simply stood by, doing nothing. Kuschka overheard that some men had ripped wooden slats from a fence to beat the prisoner. One person interjected: "But he was an airman in an enemy bomber!" Others called the act a cowardly murder. Hans Hunger, a man who lived nearby in a single-family home on Friedrich-Albert-Strasse (now called Pestalozzistrasse), was said to be one of the murderers. He had a young family, young boys. As Kuschka remembers, he asked himself at the time: "How could [Hunger] have been so full of hatred to kill a defenceless Canadian prisoner of war? I suddenly recognized the brutality of the Nazis and of the war, and I was disturbed for a long time." In his letter to the editor, Kuschka added that he heard at the time that Hans Hunger was a lawyer in Frankenberg and that he did not survive the war:

> By mid-April 1945, in the midst of chaos, it was said that Attorney Hunger had committed suicide with his family. (This is what people said. I don't know whether it is true or not.)

I spoke with Frau Bodenschatz again later in the fall of 2004, and asked her about this story. She said she was surprised to hear this and told me that she believes Hunger was an employee of the electrical utility company, and not a lawyer. She said that while she never heard of his suicide, he did "disappear" after the war.

However, that day in May in Frankenberg, I continued asking Frau Bodenschatz about her recollections.

"You had said earlier that the Canadian prisoner of war died of his wounds in a military hospital. What made you think that he did?"

"I only heard it from other people."

"A few years ago, you said in an interview that you had recognized the prisoner as a Canadian airman because he was wearing a maple leaf. Earlier this year, when I called you from Canada, you told me that you didn't remember actually seeing a maple leaf, and that you must have assumed that later. Did you in fact know at the time that the murdered foreign soldier was a Canadian airman?"

"Well, yes. There must have been some other way for me to realize this. I now don't recall how I found out. A lot of people were talking about it, and everybody said he was a Canadian airman. Later that day, when we were back home, I was horrified to hear my young nephew and some other kids running around in the yard with pieces of wood, shouting: 'Kill the Canadian! Kill the Canadian!' The children were play-acting what they had witnessed earlier."

Frau Bodenschatz also told me that she believes the "group around Max Florschütz," the local SA leader, was responsible for the murder.

"I believe Florschütz was taken away and somehow punished for this crime after the war, but I don't know whether it was by the Russians or later during the GDR period. At any rate, some time in the early 1960s, I was surprised to see him back in Frankenberg again. At the time, I was an employee of the *Konsum* (cooperative) at the corner of Lächenstrasse and Hohe Strasse. Max Florschütz served as a volunteer on the committee that ran the organization."

Frau Bodenschatz told me that Florschütz had died some years ago. Some months after our conversation, I received a tip that Florschütz's daughter was still alive and living at a nursing home in town. I asked my cousin to pay her a visit at the Sonnenlicht (sunlight) Home on Einsteinstrasse. He provided me with a written report.

Martha Opitz, née Florschütz, is an 88-year-old widow. From the beginning, she warned me that her memory is not particularly good when it comes to her younger years. She proudly announced that her father had been the "company commander" of the Frankenberg fire brigade and a member of the Storm Troopers [SA] Reserve. Whenever there was a special occasion such as the Sharpshooters' Festival, or some demonstration, he and two other men regularly marched through the town in SA uniform at six in the morning, loudly beating drums to wake up the people. He was also a good piano player, who liked to entertain people in restaurants and pubs. No, there had been no talk in the family about prisoners of war or the war in general.

I thanked Frau Bodenschatz for speaking with me, and for the coffee. I asked her to let me know if anything else should come to her mind later that had anything to do with the murder. I walked from the Bodenschatz apartment to the nearby railway station to meet Ulrich Köhler. It was a three-minute walk from the apartment building on Pestalozzistrasse to the corner of Amalienstrasse and Äussere Freiberger Strasse, where the murder had occurred, and another three minutes across the railway tracks to the station. Herr Köhler was waiting for me. He had come to Frankenberg from his home in Noschkowitz, near Döbeln. Köhler is two years older than I. In 1945, when I was a 13-year-old student at the high school in Frankenberg, he was a 15-year-old first-year student at the Teacher's College right next door to the high school. (At that time, elementary-teacher training started at a very young age in Germany.) We were both in the Hitler Youth — he in the senior element called "Hitlerjugend," I in the junior element called "Jungvolk." We hadn't known each other. After all, I had only arrived in Frankenberg in February 1945.

Together, we walked to the scene of the murder. In 1945, Köhler and his mother lived diagonally across the street from that corner. He confirmed what Ahnert had already reported about his recollections of the murder. He added that the Wehrmacht soldier he had seen escorting and (unsuccessfully) guarding the prisoner was an older man. Köhler is very precise in his statements and thinks carefully before answering questions. He is not inclined to speculate and not afraid to admit that he doesn't remember certain details. However, I had the feeling that what he does remember is based on fact. I found nothing contradictory in his recollections. He seemed to be a most reliable witness.

As we talked, I realized that I had left my camera at Frau Bodenschatz's apartment. Together, we walked back, and I had an opportunity to introduce the two witnesses to each other. They had never met before. Now, as the three of us went over some of the events together, I again observed that they each had their own style of responding to questions about the distant past. While Frau Bodenschatz seemed sometimes a bit reluctant to offer details and sometimes quick to confirm or retract, Ulrich Köhler appeared to be careful but confident, with apparently very accurate recall and great consistency.

I walked back to the murder site with Köhler and took some pictures from various angles. I photographed the precise spot where — according to the eyewitnesses — the airman was attacked by his assailants, and the spot across the road to which he had dragged himself. There, he lay in a pool of blood.

Later, after I had returned to Canada, I had a letter from Ulrich Köhler that added to my small collection of information about Max Florschütz. He had been talking with some of his former classmates from elementary school, and it so happens that one of them is married to a goddaughter of Florschütz's. Köhler went to see the woman. She confirmed that Max Florschütz had "walked around in SA uniform." She also said that before the war, he had been a guard in Sachsenburg concentration camp (where Köhler's father-in-law had been held prisoner). The woman seemed to know about Florschütz's alleged participation in the murder, but said that he was not prosecuted after the war because he had been "very humane."

My time in Frankenberg was running out quickly, and I had to make a decision. Should I visit Frau Braune, the other eyewitness mentioned by Ahnert? She had seen the body of the Canadian airman lying in the street after the murder. Or should I drive to the nearby village of Sachsenburg to meet the new witness, Elfriede Rupprecht, who had come forward as a result of the newspaper article? I had already talked with Frau Braune on the telephone to confirm her statement. She had told me she didn't have anything to add. Frau Rupprecht, on the other hand, seemed to have some new, interesting information. I decided to drive to Sachsenburg.

When she had responded to the recent newspaper article in the *Freie Presse*, Frau Rupprecht had already given me a few details. When I met her in person, in the comfortable apartment she shares with her husband, she elaborated.

I am now seventy-five. In March 1945, when I was 15 years old, we lived in Frankenberg. Shortly after the big bombing attack on

Eyewitness Ulrich Köhler in 1945.

The murder site at the corner of Äussere Freiberger Strasse and Amalienstrasse in Frankenberg. The ambush occurred where the two men are standing. Photo taken in May 2004.

Chemnitz on March 5 and 6, I was walking on Hindenburgstrasse with my mother and my two sisters, who were young children at the time. The youngest was in a baby carriage. We were on our way to visit my grandmother who lived on that street. We were walking uphill on the right-hand sidewalk. Shortly after we had passed the railway crossing, we met a handcuffed prisoner being escorted by one or two German soldiers. They were coming downhill on the opposite sidewalk. I saw men beating the prisoner over and over. The soldier escort told us not to stop, but to walk on. We were very upset about what happened.

When we came to my grandmother's home, we told her what we had seen. My older sister was living with my grandmother at the time. Normally, my sister would have been at work, at the Sachsenburg textile mill, but we found her at home when we arrived. When we told her what we had seen, she said that the day before (or it might have been more than a day), she and the other workers of her shift had been ordered to interrupt their work. An "American" airman had voluntarily given himself up at the factory after parachuting from a plane that had crashed. The workers were told to look at the airman, hurl abuse at him, insult him, and spit at him. My sister said that he must have been the same prisoner whose beating we had witnessed. I cannot provide any more information, but these images came back to me when I read your article. I felt sorry for the young man and was sad that I couldn't help him.

From Frau Rupprecht's description, it was clear that the location she describes as the murder scene is identical to that identified by the other witnesses. The others didn't say that the prisoner was handcuffed. Frau Rupprecht is the only witness who thinks there might have been two German soldiers escorting the Canadian. Although there is no proof of any connection, it is quite possible that the "American" who surrendered at the Sachsenburg textile mill was in fact the Canadian airman murdered in Frankenberg, about five kilometres away. It is certainly very likely that the airman insulted by the workers in Sachsenburg was taken to the closest military establishment, the nearby Frankenberg barracks.

In Germany, Canadians have been called "Americans" forever. When thousands of emigrants moved to the New World in the eighteenth and nineteenth centuries, they went to "America." After all, Canada is on the American continent. After my immigration in 1952, it took me thirteen years to save enough money to return to the country of my birth for a visit. I remember constantly correcting people in Germany when they asked me how I liked living in America.

"I don't live in America, I live in Canada."

"What's the difference? Canada is in North America, isn't it?"

"Yes, in North America. But I have become a Canadian, not an American. Americans are citizens of the United States."

It always was — and still is — difficult to convince some Europeans that Canadians are a distinct people and don't like to be called Americans.

Considering the relative obscurity of Canada and Canadians in the minds of Germans at the time of World War II, it would have been quite natural for a Canadian airman to be identified as an American. On the other hand, all English-speaking Allies, whether British, Canadian, or Australian, were almost always lumped together as *Engländer* (Englishmen). Among the bombers that crashed during the attack on Chemnitz on March 5/6,

Eyewitness Elfriede Rupprecht.

1945, was a Lancaster from 460 Squadron. The pilot, RAAF Squadron Leader John Holmes (DFC), six other Australians, and one RAF airman were killed. Over their common grave, the Germans erected a cross with the inscription "*Hier ruhen 8 englische Flieger …*" (Here rest 8 English airmen …) The fact that the airman captured at the Sachsenburg textile mill was referred to as an "American" certainly does not preclude him from having been the "unknown Canadian airman."

As my trip to Germany came to an end, I was still quite disappointed. I had learned more details. I was as convinced as ever that the murder actually took place, that the murder victim had been a young Canadian airman, and that the crime had been a planned, premeditated operation that must have required some collaboration between the actual perpetrators and someone in a position of authority at the Frankenberg army barracks. The men with their wooden clubs did not happen to be at the street corner at precisely the time when the Canadian prisoner and his escort walked by. Someone must have informed them that he was going to be taken to the railway station at that time. They positioned themselves at the right place at a predetermined time.

My briefcase was full: photocopies of numerous archival documents, many memos and interview notes, and several films to be developed. However, the murder victim was still the "unknown Canadian airman," killed on an unknown date by alleged perpetrators. His body had been moved to an unknown destination. I still wasn't sure whether he had belonged to a bomber crew or whether he had parachuted from an escort fighter. What, for example, had happened to the fighter that collided with the Lancaster piloted by Ross over Chemnitz? There was so much more work to be done.

CHAPTER 9

Terror Flyers

During my visit to Germany, I learned something about the bombing of Chemnitz, the murder in Frankenberg, and the disposal of the victim's body. However, I still hadn't learned the identity of the victim. I wondered whether I should start preparing myself for the arduous task of searching every Allied cemetery in Germany hoping to come across a Canadian airman whose grave was moved from Frankenberg on December 8, 1948.

My main objective was to find the name of the murdered Canadian — and thus the location of his grave. In the process, I also learned more about the murder of airmen in general.

There is no doubt whatsoever that in World War II, the murder of POWs was considered a war crime and was a violation of the Geneva Convention.

Article 2 of the Geneva Convention on the Treatment of Prisoners of War, dated July 27, 1929, ratified by Germany in 1934, states that:

Prisoners of war are in the power of the hostile Government, but not of the individuals or formation which captured them.

They shall at all times be humanely treated and protected, particularly against acts of violence, from insults and from public curiosity. Measures of reprisal against them are forbidden.

Of course, the wholesale slaughter of civilians (including women and children) by aerial bombardment is a violation as well. But it is not my purpose here to consider whether one particular violation was worse than another. I leave this argument to ethicists, philosophers, experts in international law and human rights, and especially to the reader. It is difficult to remain unemotional about brutality, whether it is encountered on a personal level (as in the murder of a POW) or on an "impersonal," military level (as in "strategic" bombing).

Hundreds of Allied airmen were murdered in Germany after being taken prisoner following bombing raids. One conservative estimate puts the number of murdered Canadian airmen between February 1 and April 30, 1945, at only seven.[1] A much larger number of victims is given by the German Web site, Willi Wachholz's *Flieger-Lynchmorde im Zweiten Weltkrieg* (www.flieger-lynchmorde.de). It documents 314 cases of Allied airmen murdered on former German territory between July 1943 and May 1945. This figure includes 26 Canadians (one of whom was erroneously identified as R.B. Denison, murdered in Frankenberg). Over the course of my research for this book I came across evidence of another ten or more murders of Canadian airmen during this period (see Appendix IV).

Did German civilians kill Allied airmen — commonly called *Terrorflieger* (terror flyers) — because they were outraged by the indiscriminate bombing of civilian targets, and of their own homes? No doubt some did. Grief over dead family members and outrage over destroyed homes and lost possessions may have motivated some people to act violently. However, there is reason to believe that most of these crimes were not committed impulsively by an aroused citizenry, but by officials who either acted under orders or who believed that they were correctly interpreting the directives from their leadership, "not to interfere with violence," as a licence to kill. It is clear that these orders were intended to produce exactly such an interpretation.

This hypothesis — that most of the murders of Allied POWs were planned rather than spontaneous — is supported by the following facts. The list of Canadian airmen known to have been murdered between July 1944 and April 1945 (see Appendix IV) attributes only one case directly to civilians: the Frankenberg murder. Of course, the eyewitness reports indicate that even the Frankenberg murder was actually a planned attack. At least two of the suspects in that case were Nazi officials. Virtually all the murders included in this list are attributed to perpetrators who were men in some official capacity: the military (Wehrmacht) and paramilitary (Volkssturm), the Storm Troopers and the SS, the Gestapo and other police forces. One of these murders was committed by a teacher and his students, which also suggests an organized effort rather than spontaneous action. One Canadian airman was murdered by a *Förster* (forest warden). In five cases it isn't known whether or not the perpetrators were civilians or officials of one kind or another.

Another case, not included in Wachholz's list, is a sad and well-documented event which occurred on March 24/25, 1944. Gestapo and SS troops murdered six RCAF flight lieutenants who were recaptured after the "great escape" from the Stalag (POW camp) at Sagan (today called Zagan) in Lower Silesia. Together with 44 other Allied airmen, they were stood against a wall and shot. Thus almost all the Canadian airmen in this small but significant sample were murdered by German soldiers, Nazi and police officers, and other officials, rather than "spontaneously" by outraged civilians.

The Nazi media, which were under the complete control of

Josef Goebbels, Reich Minister for National Enlightenment and Propaganda, had invented and widely publicized some special terms to describe the bombing of civilian targets. Allied air operations were called *Terrorangriffe* (terrorist raids) or *Terrorhandlungen* (terrorist activities). The bomber crews were called *Terrorflieger* (terror flyers or terrorist airmen). Needless to say, no one in Germany used such terminology in connection with German bombing raids against cities in England.

Initially, the German police had taken action to prevent or contain any threats or transgressions by German civilians against airmen or other prisoners of war. However, in August 1943, Heinrich Himmler, the man in charge of the SS and all police forces in Germany, issued orders "not to intervene in arguments" with enemy airmen. On May 28, 1944, Goebbels published an article in the *Völkischer Beobachter*, the Nazi Party daily newspaper, under the heading "*Zum Luftterror*" (air-raid terrorism). In it, Goebbels suggested the creation of a safety valve by allowing civilians themselves to punish Allied airmen whose planes were shot down or who had an emergency landing: "An eye for an eye, a tooth for a tooth."[2] In June 1944 he issued a decree that classified attacks by low-flying planes against civilians, passenger trains, hospitals, etc., as terrorist acts that justified the "lynching" of any airmen who had committed such acts. Captured Allied pilots already in the collection camp at Oberursel (in the Taunus Region), who had allegedly participated in the "terrorist bombing," were to be handed over to the SS Security Service for "special treatment" (that is, execution). After the *Aussenamt* [Foreign Ministry] and the *Oberkommando der Luftwaffe* [Air Force High Command] agreed, this procedure was followed with some consistency. Numerous cases of "murder by execution" were later tried before Allied courts. Those convicted were sentenced to death and executed.[3]

There is ample evidence that Himmler, Goebbels, and other top Nazi leaders encouraged the murder of Allied "terror flyers" and even issued orders to the SS, the SS Security Service, and the

Gestapo to execute Allied airmen under certain circumstances. However, it would be inaccurate to draw the conclusion from this that the Nazis ever ordered civilians to murder prisoners of war. Certainly the men who murdered the Canadian airman in Frankenberg had no such orders. Yet it is likely that the perpetrators felt their deed would go unpunished, that it would be ignored or even condoned by Nazi authorities, especially in the chaotic final phase of the war. However, they must have known that it was a shadowy area, and for that reason they took precautions to hide their own identity and to cover up the murder by having the body buried without identification.

At the Nuremberg Trials held in 1945/46 by the International Military Tribunal, several of the men tried as major war criminals were questioned about the murder and execution of Allied airmen and other prisoners of war. Excerpts from the trial transcripts, as quoted in the Avalon Project of Yale Law School (see below), indicate that numerous orders in this regard were issued not only by Hitler, Himmler, and Goebbels, but also by members of the Wehrmacht High Command: General Field Marshal Keitel, Colonel General Jodl, and Major General Warlimont. Keitel and Jodl were convicted of numerous crimes and sentenced to death by hanging.

War Crimes and Crimes against Humanity; Crimes against Military Personnel; Lynching of Allied Airmen. On 21 May 1944 Keitel received a note from WFST [Wehrmacht Operations Staff] to the effect that Hitler had decided that enemy fliers who had been forced down should be shot without court-martial, if they had engaged in "acts of terror." Keitel wrote on the note "Please arrange for order to be drafted. K."

On 17 June 1944 Keitel wrote to the Foreign Office to ask their approval of the proposed measure and the agreed definition of "Acts of Terror." On the same day Keitel wrote to Göring to ask for his approval of the definitions of "Acts of

Terror," and also to ask that he give verbal instructions to the Commandant of the camp at Oberursel to hand over fliers guilty of such acts to the SD. Both Keitel and Jodl initialed this letter. Göring replied that fliers not guilty of acts of terror must be protected, and suggested that such matters be handled by the courts.[4]

Hermann Göring, who had been a fighter pilot in World War I and was in charge of the Luftwaffe arm of the Wehrmacht, is the only senior Nazi on record to have opposed the murder of Allied airmen. However, although he had once been Hitler's second-in-command, his influence with the Führer had already waned greatly toward the end of the war. Under pressure from Hitler himself, he agreed to the execution of those "terror flyers" who had committed quite narrowly defined acts of "aerial terrorism." Göring was also found guilty at Nuremberg, on several counts, and sentenced to death. He escaped hanging by committing suicide.

In spite of the orders there were many cases in which Germans — civilians and soldiers — treated downed airmen fairly and humanely, even in the wake of the firestorms. I was to come across several such stories in the course of my investigation.

This account comes from a letter I received from Ursula Stopp in Ehrenfriedersdorf (in the Ore Mountains), who participated in the questioning of a Canadian airman after the major attacks on Dresden of February 13/14, 1945. While attending an interpreters' school in Dresden, the 18-year-old girl had survived the firestorm. Her school and the house where she had been staying were destroyed. She was buried in the cellar for hours, and she lost all her belongings. After her rescue, and after witnessing horrendous scenes of death and destruction, she joined a trek of desperate refugees leaving the city. After surviving yet another attack in the outskirts of Dresden, she finally made her way back to her home village of Mildenau in the upper Ore Mountains.

Shortly after I arrived home in the evening, my village was also attacked by bombers. The church was hit and gutted. Several farms, the lace-making school and the village's only industry, the stocking factory, were destroyed. Until then, the people in the village had felt safe, since there was no military presence whatsoever. There were no worthwhile targets at all, just the poor villagers eking out a modest living under harsh conditions high up in the Ore Mountains. I noticed that some French prisoners of war were helping to put the fires out.

In the morning of February 15, I was summoned to the Mayor's office to interpret. There, I was presented to an RCAF airman. He was good-looking, but his uniform was a dirty mess. He had been captured the night before. His manner was very polite and open; he shook hands with the Mayor (who was also the local Nazi Party leader) and with me. He said that he was a bricklayer, married, with two children. He told me I resembled his wife, and he showed me a photo. He asked me whether the Mayor was a Nazi. Of course, I couldn't say no. He was obviously surprised about his humane treatment. He asked whether he could get something to read, and then whether he could take a bath. He certainly needed one, but he had the wrong idea about conditions in this little mountain village. I don't know whether anyone there had a bathroom.

He asked about the other crew members and was told that he, the rear gunner, was the sole survivor, as far as we knew at the time. He was very upset, put his right hand over his heart and said: "They were good buddies." His own injuries seemed to be minor ... I went home to find some reading material for him, an English-language magazine called "Around the World." When I came back, he had already been moved. I never heard from him again. I believe that those few minutes in Mildenau might have been the best part of his imprisonment. He had been treated correctly, even though the people had just suffered terribly from the bombing.

Günter Assmann is an amateur historian in Freiberg, Saxony. His particular interest is the Allied bombing of Saxon cities in 1944/45.[5] He has collected much relevant documentation as well as some anecdotal information. He believes that the plane that crashed near Mildenau was Halifax III *MZ-422*, coded *ZL-N*, of 427 Squadron. According to RCAF records, three crew members (Sergeant H. Mayer, Flight Sergeant A. Williams and Sergeant A. Morrison) survived that crash. Mildenau is just northeast of Annaberg.

A British airman, rear gunner Joe Williams, related his experience on March 5, 1945. His plane had lost an engine on the climb, after it took off from its base at Kelstern in Lincolnshire. Although the damaged bomber was unable to reach the scheduled altitude of 18,000 feet, the pilot decided to proceed to the target: Chemnitz. They found little flak over Chemnitz, and the city was glowing in the light of many fires. As the bombs were released, Williams spotted a German night fighter attacking them from below.

The cannon shells came banging in all along the fuselage. Both wings were ablaze and the tail plane [horizontal stabilizer] was falling off in lumps.[6]

Williams parachuted and landed on snow-covered ground, with painful burns. He buried his parachute and Mae West (a yellow life jacket inflatable by means of carbon dioxide cartridges, named after the voluptuous actress) and walked to an isolated farm house, where he knocked on the door to give himself up, shouting "*Engländer.*"

The family was roused, and they were really kind. They gave me a drink of water, pointed to my burns, and suggested "benzine," to which I agreed … The son was sent to fetch the Volkssturm, and they arrived in slouch hats, carrying shot-guns — just like our Home Guard … Next day … I was taken to a doctor … [who] treated my face …

Williams was eventually taken to Chemnitz and, together with other POWs, put on a train for Nuremberg.

The city [Chemnitz] had been bombed, and a hostile crowd gathered round us. To their credit our young guards cocked their Tommy guns and the crowd left us alone.

I later learned that Williams was a crew member in Lancaster I *NG240* CF-12 (from 625 Squadron), whose pilot, RCAF Flying Officer J.W. Alexander, decided to keep flying after the plane was severely damaged and on fire. Eventually, the crew, including two Canadians, all bailed out safely. Incredibly, the aircraft finally crashed far to the north, on the island of Rügen off the Baltic coast.[7]

On the other hand, some stories by Germans about their own acts of humanity in the midst of madness, told long after the war, should perhaps be regarded with some caution. It would have been extremely dangerous to disobey orders in a situation as described in the following account:

In 1944, I was drafted from high school near Munich to man anti-aircraft defences against Allied bombers. Following a heavy raid, I was ordered to round up a bomber crew who had bailed out over a nearby forest. As we were taking the wounded men into custody, an SS fanatic roared up in a Mercedes and started shooting with a Schmeisser machine pistol. I smashed the butt of my K-98 rifle against his skull, knocking him cold. When we reached the safety of the command post, a Canadian prisoner named Lt. Cowing asked my name. After the armistice, I received a surprise summons from the POW commander: "You're being released early because some Canadian airman filed a report about you."[8]

It would have taken an almost unbelievable amount of courage to stand up to an SS man in this way. Certainly the German soldier who stood by that day in Frankenberg while the Canadian prisoner of war in his charge was beaten to death showed no such courage.

CHAPTER 10

Eureka!

This search had begun as an interest and grown into a pre-occupation. Was it becoming a fixation? A war crime, an atrocity, had been committed. A young life had ended in violence. Justice had not been done, and the Department of National Defence bureaucrats in Canada had forgotten the deed. The war crimes report — such as it was — had been filed away, and neither the victim nor the perpetrators were ever identified. I felt a strong, internal force urging me to search, to dig, to ask questions, to tell, to write, to e-mail, to telephone. Everything I saw, heard, or read forced me to think of that lost Canadian murdered in the streets of Frankenberg. Philip Roth expressed it so well:

> This is what happens when you write books. There's not just something that drives you to find out everything — something begins putting everything in your path. There is suddenly no such thing as a back road that doesn't lead headlong into your obsession.[1]

There were also times of doubt. Should I be doing this? I had no experience in detective work, although it was not unlike other historical research I had done. But was I methodical enough? Or was I overlooking some essential avenues, key sources, crucial archival collections?

Should I have tried harder to find the mysterious Alfred Hermann Paul who had informed the British war crimes commission in 1945? My Internet search for him had come up empty. Should I have tried harder to locate the witness Paul had mentioned, Dr Ka(a)tz? In both cases, I had gone no farther than searching the Internet and Leipzig address and telephone books.

I had encountered *eureka* moments before, in other historical research projects when after a lengthy and sometimes frustrating search through records and books, the solution to a puzzle suddenly presented itself. I needed such a breakthrough in this case. I needed serendipity.

On June 4, 2004, going over my numerous Frankenberg papers once again, I found a note to myself that I hadn't yet acted upon. It read, "Ask CWGC to locate Matthew Orr's grave." Of course! Orr's body had been moved from the Frankenberg cemetery to an unknown location on December 8, 1945, the same day on which the unknown airman's grave was moved. I immediately sent another e-mail to the Commonwealth War Graves Commission in Maidenhead: "Can you find where the British soldier Matthew Orr is buried?"

Two days later, Emily Bird of the CWG told me that Matthew Orr's grave had been located at the Allied War Cemetery on Heerstrasse in Berlin-Charlottenburg. Then, in the late evening of June 11, 2004, I opened the following e-mail:

Following your fresh information regarding this casualty being moved together with Matthew Orr, I was able to trace him immediately.

No unknown were transferred from Frankenberg to the Berlin War Cemetery. However, alongside Orr, the only exhumation from Frankenberg was the following casualty. I must assume that this is the casualty to whom you refer as all the details given match those which you provided.

Casualty: P/O HENRI JEAN MAURICE JOSEPH D'AVRIL, J/93925
Served With: 425 Sqdn. Royal Canadian Air Force
Died: 5th March 1945, grave number: 13. C. 7
Additional Information: Age 22
Son of Henri and Cecile D'Avril, of Montreal, Province of Quebec, Canada.

Please feel free to contact me if I can be of any further assistance.
Yours sincerely,
Emily Bird, Enquiries Section

Eureka! The great moment had arrived! The moment I had been hoping and waiting for. On June 11, less than four months after my investigation began, I had found the "unknown" Canadian airman's name and service number. He was a 22-year-old French Canadian from Montreal. I immediately checked the list of Canadian casualties for March 5/6, 1945, on Richard Koval's Web site. Sure enough, there he was, "F/Sgt H. D'Avrill" (notwithstanding the misspelling of D'Avril and the fact that his rank was given as flight sergeant instead of pilot officer). D'Avril was listed as a casualty of the Halifax III *PN-173*, coded *KW-Q*, one of the Six Group planes that failed to return from Germany that night. The bomber's crew was all Canadian, and two others were also listed as casualties of that last flight, the pilot, F/O J. Desbien, and P/O A. Minguet. The other four, F/Sgt G. Tremblay, F/O J. Parent, F/Sgt G. Langevin, and F/Sgt L. Lamontagne, were taken prisoner.

Why hadn't I followed up on this particular plane and its crew? I had known for a long time that this Halifax was among the six bombers that failed to return from the raid on Chemnitz. But until now, I was still speculating that the most likely victim was Flight Lieutenant Ross, pilot of the RCAF Lancaster that had crashed near Königshain.

For a short moment after discovering the name of the "unknown Canadian airman," I was tempted to rest on my laurels and end the investigation right there. I had reached my main goal: to find the identity of the Frankenberg murder victim. But I couldn't stop now. I immediately prepared for three more tasks: to find out how his identity had been discovered, to order his personnel file at Library and Archives Canada, and to locate the crash site of his plane. Also in the back of my mind was the hope that I might find some living relatives.

I wrote to Maidenhead, thanked Emily Bird for her help, and asked her for more details. In particular, could it be confirmed that D'Avril's exhumed body was brought to Berlin from Frankenberg? This would prove beyond the shadow of a doubt that he was indeed the murder victim. And how was the CWGC able to identify the body as that of D'Avril? According to the Frankenberg records, the body had been buried in Frankenberg as an "unknown Canadian airman who died as a prisoner of war." The Germans who had buried and then reburied the body in Frankenberg either hadn't known his identity or did not wish to reveal it due to the circumstances of his death. Was an unmistakable identification made when Allied authorities exhumed the body in Frankenberg on December 8, 1948? Would any records have been kept of this exhumation and reburial? If so, are these records available?

Emily Bird confirmed right away that D'Avril's body had indeed been moved to Berlin from Frankenberg on December 8, 1945, and that he had previously been buried there as an unknown Canadian airman. There was now no doubt that he was the murdered Canadian airman:

Temporary grave marker erected at Berlin War Cemetery, c. 1949.

He was found with a marker on his grave that read "*Hier ruht ein unbekannter kanadischer Soldat, der noch in der Kriegsgefangenschaft sein Leben lassen musste.*" When the graves concentration unit exhumed his body to move him to the Berlin War Cemetery, they found his identity disc.

I then asked for written confirmation that the identity of the "unknown Canadian airman" was clearly established as that of Henri Jean-Maurice Joseph D'Avril, with the date of the identification. On June 16, 2004, I received a fax from the Commonwealth War Graves Commission in Maidenhead confirming all that I had been told.

After D'Avril's remains had been moved from Frankenberg to Berlin in December 1948, a temporary marker in the shape of a cross was placed on the grave. At that time, the war cemetery was still under construction, and no lawn had yet been laid.

Throughout my investigation, I had kept in touch with Dr Koch in Berlin. I sent him occasional updates and called him on the telephone now and then. He was one of the first with whom I shared the good news about my discovery. In October 2004, Dr Koch went to the cemetery where he found and photographed the grave and its surroundings for me.

The Berlin War Cemetery, 1939–1945, lies in a quiet forest setting on the south side of Heerstrasse in Berlin-Charlottenburg, about eight kilometres west of the city's centre. The district of Charlottenburg came to be part of the British sector when the city was divided in 1945. The cemetery is well-kept, with neat rows of white gravestones among green lawns. Flowers have been planted and are maintained around the gravestones. A sign at the entrance reads: "Here lie the bodies of British and Allied soldiers, sailors and airmen who died in Berlin during the Second World War. Great Britain 2680, Canada 527, Australia 223, New Zealand 56, South Africa 31, India 50, Poland 5, unknown 8, total 3,580." The sign is not entirely correct in that many of the 3,580 military personnel buried there, including Jean-Maurice D'Avril, did not die in Berlin, but their bodies were brought to the cemetery from other parts of the former East Germany after the war. At the top of Jean-Maurice D'Avril's stone is the RCAF crest. In the middle is the following inscription, in a curious mixture of French and English:

Officier-Pilote
H.J.M.J. D'AVRIL
Wireless Operator Air Gunner
Royal Canadian Air Force
Le 5 Mars 1945 Age 22

At the bottom of the stone, under a large cross, and partly hidden by plants, are the words:

Here we cry with heart's endeavour,
grant him rest that is for ever.
Dad, Mother, Sister

CHAPTER 11

Here We Cry

Knowledge of the murder victim's identity accelerated my investigation. I called Library and Archives Canada in Ottawa and ordered D'Avril's personnel file.[1] At the archives the next day, I carefully read every document in the file. Throughout the process, I felt as if I were indirectly communicating with the young man whose murder remains officially unrecognized and unpunished.

We have a son in his early twenties. Now, when I look at him, I cannot help thinking of Jean-Maurice D'Avril. What would our son have done had he lived in the Canada of World War II? He might well have joined the RCAF and served under Bomber Command. He might have volunteered, considering it his patriotic duty. If he had, he would have followed orders with a clear conscience, believing in a righteous cause. He would have performed his tasks to the best of his ability. I would like to think that — given a choice — our son would have refused to kill thousands of innocent women and children by firebombing their homes. But

Jean-Maurice's father, Henri D'Avril (1898–1988).

no one would have given him that choice. Our son would have climbed aboard his bomber with the rest of the crew and performed his duties. As Jean-Maurice D'Avril did. If our son's plane had been hit in the midst of the hell and confusion that was the sky over Chemnitz on March 5, 1945, if he had bailed out and landed somewhere in the snow, he would have been happy to have survived. He would have surrendered and hoped that he could trust the enemy soldiers to treat him as fairly as he would have treated one of their own under the same circumstances. And if some political fanatics had attacked him and smashed his skull with wooden clubs, he would have died a miserable death in the street, as Jean-Maurice D'Avril did. My wife and I would have grieved for him as Jean-Maurice D'Avril's parents grieved for their only son.

The young man's full name was Henri Jean-Maurice Joseph D'Avril. In documents in his personnel file at the archives, his name appears in various forms, but he always signed his papers "Jean-Maurice D'Avril." From these documents and other sources I learned many facts about his short life.

Jean-Maurice was born in Montreal on February 21, 1923, the son of Henri D'Avril, a French citizen (from St Pierre and Miquelon), and Cecile, née Duffy, of St Calixte, Quebec. Before enlisting in the RCAF at age 19, he lived with his parents at 4603 Chabot Street, Montreal. The family was Roman Catholic and belonged to the congregation of St-Pierre-Claver Church in Montreal. He attended Ecole St-Pierre-Claver, and

Jean-Maurice's mother, Cecile D'Avril, née Duffy (1898–1969).

Jean-Maurice (front row, second from right) and his swim team at the Palestre Nationale in Montreal.

completed his formal education at Ecole Supérieure St-Stanislas, attaining senior matriculation in 1942. He participated in all school sports. He excelled at swimming. He was a cadet drummer for two years, and a boy scout. After graduation, he went to work for Canadian Liquid Air in Montreal. He could type and drive a car. He bowled, played tennis, ping-pong and baseball; he enjoyed fishing.

On October 23, 1942, Jean-Maurice D'Avril presented himself to the No.13 RCAF Recruiting Centre in Montreal. He was judged able to speak English

Jean-Maurice as a cadet drummer, with little sister Lise.

"fairly well" (no mention of French, his mother tongue). The officer who conducted the first basic test, Flying Officer Lambert, found the young recruit "suitable for aircrew." D'Avril was 70 ¼ inches (175 cm) tall and weighed 166 pounds (75 kg), his visual acuity was 20/20/20/30. His blood type was A. The medical officer, too, categorized him as "good material." He was finally interviewed by Flight Lieutenant Gibeault, who assessed him as:

Tall — athletic — good appearance — good general background — well qualified culturally and educationally for his future war services — keen on training for aircrew duties — would like to be a fighter pilot, preferably — well disciplined — good material.

On November 18, 1942, Jean-Maurice was accepted into the RCAF. He began basic training in Montreal, and from there attended a number of training facilities in Ontario and Quebec over the next 16 months, gaining the skills needed for air warfare. He was, in the words of Chief Instructor Flight Lieutenant J.W. Kennedy, an "above average worker — keen personality, intelligent, determined to succeed."

On March 25, 1944, he embarked at Halifax for Britain and disembarked at Greenock, Scotland, eight days later. Training continued in England, where he eventually specialized as a W/O (wireless operator). The school's commanding officer rated him, "an above average W/O who has displayed great keenness in his training with good results. Crew co-operation good. Suitable for early recommendation to commissioned rank." Upon completion, September 20, 1944, he was posted to 61 Base. On November 14, he was promoted to flight sergeant (T/F/S), and on December 2, he finally joined 425 (Alouette) Squadron.

The personnel file contains two photos of Jean-Maurice D'Avril. One, in which he wears a peaked RCAF wedge cap at a rakish angle, may have been taken shortly after his enlistment, since no insignia or rank is visible on his uniform jacket. It shows a serious young man with handsome, regular features and a somewhat contemplative look in his bright eyes. He is no longer a boy, but seems not yet quite comfortable in his role. The other photo was taken later, after he earned his wing as a wireless operator/air gunner. It shows him without a cap, revealing a full head of dark hair. He looks smart in his uniform. His manly face, with the strong, freshly shaven chin, shows more determination than in the first picture.

On February 4, 1945, Jean-Maurice received his commission as Pilot Officer.

On March 7, 1945, at 12:40 a.m., Jean-Maurice D'Avril's father received a telephone call informing him that his son was missing. On the following day a telegram from an RCAF casualties officer arrived.

It was not until October 31, 1945, following frantic requests for information by the father, that the Air Ministry in London wrote to the RAF Search Bureau of the Allied Control Commission for Germany (British Element), referring to "Casualty Enquiry No. G.195." Wing Commander J.S. Harris, signing for the Air Officer Commanding-in-Chief, RCAF Overseas, told the Search Bureau that D'Avril's plane was reported missing on the night of the attack on Chemnitz. "Returned Prisoners of War believe that three of the crew members were killed. They also state the aircraft crashed around Marienberg, approximately 33 kilometres south of Chemnitz." Wing Commander Harris requested that the Search Bureau make "a search ... of the area to ascertain their fate and to obtain burial particulars."

A week later, on November 7, 1945, the RCAF Casualty Officer at the Department of National Defence for Air in Ottawa sent a registered letter to Henri D'Avril and assured him that something would now be done: "In view of the lapse of time and the absence of any further information, the Air Ministry Overseas now proposes to take action to presume for official purposes the death of your son ..." This time, the bureaucratic form letter at least contained a closing sentence, "assuring the members of your family of my earnest sympathy in this time of great anxiety." A Certificate of Presumption of Death was issued on November 29, 1945, signed

Jean-Maurice after enlist-ment in the RCAF.

by Records Officer Group Captain T.K. McDougall. A week later, the Canadian Pension Commission in Ottawa advised the pension medical examiner in Montreal that Henri D'Avril, as next of kin, was entitled to receive $60 a month for the loss of his only son.

Months later, the family was still harbouring some hope. A cousin of D'Avril's, serving with the Canadian Army Staff in Brussels at the time, wrote this appeal for help, dated January 15, 1946.

To whom it may concern:
I would like some information about a sgt. in the air force. He was considered lost in January or February 1945 … He is my cousin. His parents do not believe him to be dead, but might have lost his memory. I would appreciate an immediate attention to this letter. Thank you.
Mrs. L. Laperrière

The file contains no record of a reply.

On February 1, 1946, Henri D'Avril sent the following letter to Squadron Leader G.B. Philbin, RCAF Overseas.

Padre Laplante of the 425th Squadron gave me your address and told me to write you and ask if you would please investigate the disappearance of my son, Henri Jean Maurice D'Avril, who has been missing since March 5th,

Jean-Maurice after he earned his half-wing as wireless operator/air gunner.

1945. I am listing below all the information we have in connection with his disappearance.

F/Sgt. D'Avril No. R 202453 was promoted Pilot Officer in February and his number was changed to J93925, but it seems that his promotion had not been confirmed at the date he was listed as missing. His plane got into trouble on March 5th near Chemnitz, three of the crew jumped first and then he jumped and one man jumped after he did, they of course did not see him after he jumped, but all four of them have been found and have returned home.

If there is anything that you could possibly do for my wife and myself who still refuse to believe that he is dead, as no trace has ever been found of him, we would greatly appreciate anything that you might be in a position to do for us ...

This letter has a stamp indicating that it was received on April 2, 1946. There is no record of a reply. Instead, the next communication of record to Mr D'Avril is a letter dated May 13, 1946, from the National Defence Estates Branch telling him that his son's belongings, which had been shipped from England, would be forwarded in a few days, "in one carton by prepaid express." An inventory list in the personnel file shows that the effects were not received by Henri D'Avril until August 5, 1946.

On November 2, 1946, the DND Estates Branch in Ottawa informed Mr D'Avril that they had Jean-Maurice's diary in their possession:

Your son's diary, which was extracted from his personal belongings for censoring, is now available for forwarding to you and will be sent within the next few days by registered mail ... Any delay in sending you the diary is sincerely regretted.

A letter written on February 20, 1947, by Wing Commander W.A. Dicks, signing for the Chief of Air Staff in Ottawa, informed

Mr D'Avril that he would soon be sent the Operational Wings and Certificate "in recognition of the gallant services rendered by your son ... I realize there is little which may be said or done to lessen your sorrow, but it is my hope that these 'Wings,' indicative of operations against the enemy, will be a treasured memento of a young life offered on the altar of freedom in defence of his Home and Country." The French translator chose to render the English phrase "a young life" more poetically as "*une vie encore à son printemps*."

On November 10, 1947, the Air Ministry in London notified the RCAF Overseas Headquarters in Ottawa that the Germans had recovered only two bodies from the wreckage of the Halifax, but no trace had been found of D'Avril. The writer asked Ottawa to forward copies of survivor statements from the four crew members who were taken prisoner and then returned to Canada. The letter also stated that normally the wireless operator/air gunner is "the first to bail out." In the meantime, an investigation report dated October 17, 1947, and received by the Air Ministry a month later, on November 17, 1947, contained some of the relevant facts: The plane (erroneously identified in the report as a Lancaster) had crashed between Drebach and Herold. This was a more accurate description of the crash site than in the report of October 31, 1945, which had stated that the plane crashed "near Marienberg."

No explosion was heard but pieces of aircraft were found scattered over a wide area. The aircraft wreckage lay for some time on the scene of the crash, but has since completely disappeared, having been removed piece by piece by the civilian population.

The report cites two unnamed witnesses, interviewed at Drebach, who stated that only two bodies were found at the scene of the crash. The dead were identified by the police who had found and secured their papers. The bodies were taken to Drebach and buried in the local cemetery, "in a collective grave marked by a cross ..."

Drebach is a village about 10 kilometres west of Marienberg and about 25 kilometres south of Frankenberg, in the northern Ore Mountains. The village meanders for about five kilometres along a hilly road and a railway line. Herold is a small hamlet about 3 kilometres west of Drebach.

Records I had seen at the Frankenberg municipal archives indicated that the "unknown Canadian airman" had been exhumed and his grave moved on December 8, 1948. I knew from the War Graves Commission that D'Avril's body had been identified in the process and moved to Berlin. According to the RCAF Exhumation Report in the personnel file, the exhumation was actually performed on December 6, 1948, by Major Evan Ralphs, witnessed by RAF Squadron Leader J.W. Willis-Richards. The Major had used the "airman's disc" (identity tag) inscribed "AVRIL, H.J.D. R.C.A.F. R.202453" for identification.

It is surprising that it apparently never occurred to anyone in the RCAF or the RAF or any other Canadian or British defence authorities to investigate how, and under what circumstances, the Canadian airman — whose body was clearly identifiable even after three-and-a-half years in the grave — had died in Frankenberg and why he had been buried there as "nameless."

It took the RCAF five months to notify Jean-Maurice D'Avril's family of the exhumation, identification, and reburial of their son's body. On May 6, 1949, Wing Commander W.R. Gunn, Casualty Officer for the Chief of Air Staff, wrote to Mr D'Avril to inform him that his son's body had been located.

Dear Mr. D'Avril:
I deeply regret having to again refer to the loss of your son, Pilot Officer Henri Jean Maurice Joseph D'Avril, but a further report has been received from our Missing Research and Enquiry Service. Continued investigations in the Chemnitz area resulted in finding your son's grave. His grave was located in the cemetery at Frankenberg which is seven miles North

North East of Chemnitz. Exhumation was carried out resulting in his identification through his identity discs. It can only
be assumed that your son bailed out before the aircraft
crashed and at too low an altitude for his parachute to open.

In accordance with the agreed policy of the Nations of the
British Commonwealth that all British aircrew buried in
Germany would be moved to British Military Cemeteries
located in Germany, your son was moved to the permanent
British Military Cemetery eight miles East from the centre
of Berlin. The cemetery is known as the Berlin (Heerstrasse)
British Military Cemetery. Your son was laid to rest in Plot
13, Row C, Grave No. 7. His crewmates lie at rest beside him
in adjacent graves.

This British Military Cemetery will be reverently cared
for and maintained in perpetuity by the Imperial War
Graves Commission (of which Canada is a member). The
cemetery will be beautified by the planting of trees, shrubs
and flowers, and the Commission will also erect a permanent headstone at your son's grave.

It is my earnest hope that you will be comforted with the
knowledge that your son's resting place is known, and that it
will be permanently maintained, and I would like to take this
opportunity of expressing to you and the members of your
family my deepest sympathy in the loss of your gallant son.[2]

This letter would have dashed all hopes the family might have
harboured that their son and brother might still be alive in spite of
all odds. It was final, they had lost their only son and brother. Their
lives were changed forever. The war had left its indelible mark on
the little house on Chabot Street in Montreal, as it had on count-
less others in cities, towns, villages, and farms all over the world.[3]

CHAPTER 12

The Last Flight of the Q Queen

Jean-Maurice D'Avril probably celebrated his 22nd birthday with his air force buddies at the Tholthorpe airbase in North Yorkshire on February 21, 1945, where his RCAF squadron (425, named *Alouette*) was stationed. Alouette was the only French-Canadian squadron in Bomber Command. The bomber to which Jean-Maurice D'Avril was assigned was a Halifax III, numbered *PN-173*, coded *KW-Q*. Its crew had nicknamed it the "*Q Queen.*"

On September 27, 2004, my wife, Elizabeth, and I paid a visit to the RCAF Museum at the Canadian Forces Base on Glenn Miller Road in Trenton, Ontario. I went there to see the Halifax bomber that is being faithfully restored by a group of dedicated volunteers. Our friendly and helpful guide, Major (Ret) Charlie Hall of Brighton, Ontario, introduced us to some of the men who were working on the project that afternoon. Tom Mann, who worked as an engineer for deHavilland for 45 years, was duplicating parts for the doors to the bomb bay wing. Jack O'Donnell

says he was brought up as an air force brat. He was a police officer for 35 years. They are typical of the many volunteers who have
been piecing this giant bomber together for the past nine years,
ever since it was raised from Lake Mjosa in Norway. It had been
there at a depth of 750 feet (228 metres) for 50 years after it was
shot down by German flak (anti-aircraft fire) in April 1945, as it
was returning to England after dropping supplies for the Norwe-
gian resistance. The restoration was completed in 2005. It is the
only aircraft of its kind on display anywhere in the world. As the
brochure published by the Halifax Aircraft Association in
Toronto points out, it is meant to serve forever as a memorial to
all our airmen who died in action.[1]

This particular Halifax is not the same type as the *Q Queen*. It
is a Halifax MK VII, while D'Avril's plane was a Halifax III, an
even larger version. I was impressed by its enormous size, over-
whelming even in its incomplete state in the hangar at Trenton. It
is one thing to imagine a bomber like the Halifax III, 71 feet and
7 inches (22 metres) long, with a wing span of 104 feet (32
metres). It is quite another sensation to stand in front of its "close
relative," looking up to its nose high above the ground, and feel
absolutely dwarfed by it. The fact that near the end of World War
II, over 700, 800, or sometimes even 1,000, gigantic four-engine
Halifax and Lancaster bombers would appear over a city, dis-
gorging their deadly loads, is unimaginable to most Canadians
today. Seeing this monster on the ground brought back memories of the night in early March 1945, when Chemnitz was
destroyed in a firestorm. I was 15 kilometres away from the city
centre at the time, but the thunderous roar of the giant aircraft,
the rumble of explosions when each of the 700 bombers dropped
between 15,000 and 20,000 pounds (between 6,800 and 9,100
kilograms) of high explosives to smash the city, and the bright
red flickering shine of the fire will stay in my memory forever. I
believe that no one who ever witnessed such an attack will be able
to forget the sound. I have had many nightmares.

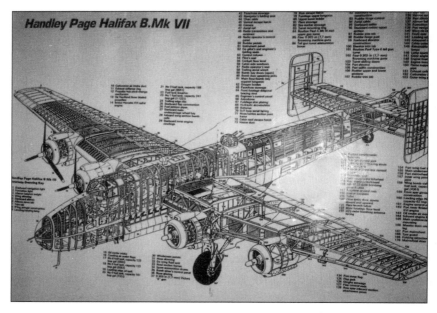

Construction drawing of a Halifax VII, restored at the RCAF Museum in Trenton, Ontario. This bomber was very similar to the Halifax III.

As Bill Tytula of the Halifax Project at the RCAF Museum in Trenton informed me, a total of 6,178 Halifax bombers were built. Parts were manufactured in 41 factories, and the planes were assembled in five different factories. The *Q Queen* was manufactured by Fairey Aviation, delivered to Tholthorpe on November 22, 1944, and taken over by 425 Squadron.

The *Q Queen* flew its first operation on February 7. However, that mission was called off, and the plane with its load of twelve 500-pound (227-kilogram) bombs landed at Carnaby before returning to its home base at Tholthorpe. This was followed by a training flight on February 10. The crew flew its first bombing mission in *KW-Q* on February 13, against the industrial complex of Böhlen and the city of Leipzig. On February 17, an operation against Wesel was called off. Between February 18 and March 3, the crew flew a number of bombing missions in *KW-Q*. The other targets — prior to Chemnitz — included the cities of

Cologne, Essen, Mainz, Mannheim, and Worms, and the town of Kamenz, northeast of Dresden.

Jean-Maurice D'Avril was the wireless operator/air gunner in his plane. The rest of the crew consisted of Flight Lieutenant Jean Jacques Desbien (the pilot, from Chicoutimi, Quebec), Flight Sergeant Albert Emile Minguet (the flight engineer, from Verdun, Quebec), Flight Sergeant George Tremblay (the navigator, from Montreal), Flying Officer Joe Parent (the bomb aimer, from Kapuskasing, Ontario), Flight Sergeant Leo Lamontagne (the mid-upper gunner from Saskatchewan), and Flight Sergeant G. Langevin (the tail gunner, from Montreal).

Twelve days after his 22nd birthday, precisely at 4:51 p.m., on March 5, 1945, D'Avril's Halifax bomber, piloted by Flight Lieutenant Jean Jacques Desbien, took off from Tholthorpe for a bombing raid on Chemnitz. It took them over four hours to reach the target.

This plane belonged to an armada of 760 Bomber Command aircraft. Twenty-six percent (198) of them were Canadian: 182 bombers from Six Group (98 Halifaxes and 84 Lancasters from a total of 15 Canadian squadrons) and 16 Pathfinders.[2]

With the help of ingenious Richard Koval, I was able to track down the last surviving crew member of the *Q Queen*, Joe Parent. On July 19, 2004, my wife and I drove almost 900 kilometres to Kapuskasing, Ontario, to interview him. Joe now resides in a seniors' residence with his wife, Suzie. He is 86 years old and uses a walker for longer distances. He can walk a short stretch and climb stairs with just the help of

Drawing of the Alouette crest by the College of Arms in January 1945. It was presented to F/S Leo Paul Lamontagne, mid-upper gunner in Halifax III PN-173, coded KW-Q, when he was still overseas.

a cane. He has a very sharp mind and excellent recall. I met him at the home of his son, Tony.

Joe's parents were from Pembroke, Ontario, but he grew up in Kirkland Lake. He had worked for a lumber company before enlisting. I transcribed Joe's account from my handwritten notes.

I enlisted in September 1942 in Kirkland Lake. At first, the RCAF wouldn't take me because I had some kind of a nose obstruction. They told me to get it fixed first. I asked them if they would pay for it, and they said no — I should have the nose fixed, and they would fix my teeth. So I had the nose done at my own expense, and then they took me and had my teeth fixed at the RCAF's expense. I was first sent to a training camp at Brandon, Manitoba. I also was at a camp in Dafoe, Saskatchewan, where I met my wife, Suzie, who was from Regina. In the spring of 1944, we were taken to England from Halifax, in the troop carrier *Andes* (not in a convoy). It took us six days to reach Liverpool. From there, we went to Bournemouth, to join a holding unit. On May 9, I arrived at Wigtown, Scotland, which was an advanced flight training camp. We trained in a twin-engine Avro Anson. On the 22nd, we were taken to a station at Stratford-on-Avon, where we trained in RCAF Wellingtons. There, I met Johnny D'Avril. We all called Jean-Maurice "John" or "Johnny." D'Avril was stressed on the first syllable (*dav*-ril). We were all speaking English, even among our own 425 Squadron, which was mostly French Canadians. He was a gentle, strong, tall man who wouldn't harm a fly. He was engaged to a girl in Montreal called Margot. He wouldn't shoot the guff or smoke or drink or go out with girls in England, and would write a letter to his girlfriend instead. Oh, he might have had one beer a week. I didn't know and Johnny may not have known that he had already received his commission as pilot officer. We all knew him only as a flight sergeant. From Stratford we were sent to a Heavy Conversion Unit at Wombleton, to train in the big four-engine Halifax.

From there, we were sent to the Bomber Command base at Tholthorpe. There were only two RCAF squadrons there: we, the 425 (Alouette) Squadron and 420 (Snowy Owl) Squadron. Our squadron commander was Group Captain Joe Lecomte.[3] We started to fly bombing missions on December 8, 1944. The Alouette Squadron was code-named KW. It consisted of 26 aircraft which were code-named from A to Z. Our Halifax was code-named *KW-Q*. We had nicknamed it the *Q Queen*, and that name was written on its nose. All planes in our squadron were Halifax III.

On the trip to Chemnitz on March 5, 1945, we were flying above the clouds. When we reached the target, we dropped our bombs through the clouds, using the H2S radar as our navigational and bomb aiming device. We didn't see the target. Johnny D'Avril was the wireless operator and air gunner. In case of evacuation, the pilot was supposed to lift the canopy above his head, and he would be sucked out with his parachute. The flight engineer was down two steps. The tail gunner bailed out through the mid-upper side door.

The plane was over the city. We carried a load of sixteen bombs at 500 pounds each, plus about 200 incendiaries. The bombs had all been armed and had started to fall when the tail gunner reported: "Corkscrew port, go, go, go!"[4] This was the signal for the pilot that we were being attacked by a fighter and that he should tip the wings. I could see the tracer bullets going by, fired by the Focke Wulf 190 behind us. He was coming at us from the top, not from the bottom as they usually did.[5] I could see our port wing on fire. The pilot said: "Put on parachutes, jump, jump, jump! Go, go go!" We all knew that there were 2,000 gallons of high-octane gas in the tanks. The bomb doors were still open. The first to bail out was Tremblay, the navigator. He just had to lift the hatch on which his stool was sitting. The second was D'Avril. He jumped just ahead of me. I didn't see D'Avril after he jumped. I don't know when Lamontagne (the mid-upper gunner) and Langevin (the tail gunner) jumped. Minguet (the flight engineer) and Desbien (the pilot) didn't make it.

It was very dark when I parachuted through the clouds. I was just wondering where the heck I was going to hit the ground. I landed in a ploughed field, in about three or four inches (eight or ten centimetres) of snow. It was very windy. I had injured my right hand: the tendons of two fingers were cut, and I was bleeding. I had also injured my hip in the fall. I headed for a clump of trees to hide in. I heard dogs barking, and thought: Holy jeepers, they have the dogs after me! Then I lit a cigarette. I spent the night in that clump of trees. I was warm enough because I was wearing an electric suit (with a plug-in for heat on the aircraft) and a heavy denim-like coverall suit with a fur collar over that. Also a Mae West. I had no survival gear. After all, I was in the Alouette Squadron, which had very little in the way of equipment. We thought we could do the same job with less. I had no compass, but I knew I had to be somewhere south of the city of Chemnitz. I used to work in the bush, and I could tell north and south. I intended to go west (not east because I didn't want to get caught by the Russians who — we were told — sometimes didn't differentiate between us and the Germans).

I hid my parachute, my Mae West, the electrical suit and the coveralls in the bushes. I was now just wearing my blue uniform, but I took the RCAF wings and the "CANADA" strip off. I thought I might perhaps be taken for a Luftwaffe airman, because they also had blue uniforms. We hadn't been briefed about what to do if we were shot down. None of us ever thought we would be shot down. It was always the other guys. At daybreak, I started walking along a road that led toward a town with a very big church. There was a stone wall around the church. I had to walk slowly because my hip hurt. I was on the road perhaps an hour and a half. I walked toward this town, and then I met a woman who was walking in the opposite direction. She said to me: *"Flieger kaputt?"* [plane broken?] At the time, I didn't know what she meant. Then I was met by three or four Volkssturm men, who shouted *"Halt!"* I knew what that meant, so I raised my arms. They took me to a building in the town that looked something like a post office. There were a lot of young fellows there who took away my cigarettes. Eventually, I was taken to Marienberg in a horse-drawn sleigh. On the sleigh, there was a driver up front and a guard inside the little sleigh. I had to sit on the floor. All along the trip, the guy pressed his revolver against my neck. It felt very cold. In Marienberg, they put me in jail, where I found three others from our crew and eight men from 415 (Swordfish) Squadron. Their plane [Halifax III *NA-204*, coded *6U-J*, piloted by W. Mitchell] had crashed too, and the whole crew was taken prisoner. So we were 11 in one room. Talk about coincidence: one of the guys from 415 Squadron (Frank Mudry) turned out to be a cousin of my girlfriend, Suzie, whom I later married. He was from Saskatchewan.

We were in Marienberg without food for four days. There were about 20 or 25 people who came looking at us. But a Russian prisoner of war or labourer or somebody like that came and threw us a dark loaf of bread. First I thought I could never eat that (I had never tasted dark bread before), but after a while, we divided it among the 11 of us, and it tasted OK. Some of the Hitler Youth boys sort of harassed us verbally and spat at us. Eventually we ended up at a place in Chemnitz.

In Chemnitz, I could still smell the stench from the burning corpses. The Volkssturm men guarding us had rifles. When we walked through the city, we were 11 POWs, and we were escorted by 11 guards. They took us to the railway station. There, a bunch of civilians crowded around us and spat at us. At one point, the guards told us to line up and face a wall. I heard when they eased the springs on their Schmeisser guns, and I thought we were going to be shot in the back. But they were protecting us from the crowd.

We were often interrogated. I tried to say that I spoke French (I thought I might be taken for a French foreign labourer), but they brought a lady who spoke better French than I did. She spoke the real French, and I had only learned French in Kirkland Lake. So we soon switched to English. I also learned a few important German words like "*scheissen*" and "*pissen*." I was given a cup of poor coffee, and then an officer interrogated me in English. He asked me whether I knew what rank he was. I told him I knew the Canadian insignia, but not the German. He asked me to guess, and I said: "Major?" He seemed a bit insulted and corrected me: "No, I'm a Colonel." He said we would be taken to a POW camp. I asked what we would be doing there, and he said not to worry, "you won't be there long enough, the war will be over soon."

We were loaded onto a train that had partly passenger cars, partly freight cars. We were first taken to a *Dulag* (transit camp) near Frankfurt, and then eventually to a much bigger camp at Moosburg near Munich. There were about 100,000 POWs at that camp. I only saw about 25 Canadians. One guard, an Austrian, was very friendly. He got bits of tobacco from other guards and rolled me some cigarettes. The Red Cross handed out food parcels that had arrived from overseas for us. It was the first real food we had for a long time. I overate and was sick. Somebody asked me: "How do you feel?" I said: "I ate like a pig, and I'm happier than hell!"

On May 6, 1945, we were liberated by Patton's Army. After some detours [According to Joe Parent's log book, they were returned to Wescott, England, via Landshut in Germany and Rheims in France] we were shipped back to England and then to Canada on the troop carrier *Louis Pasteur*. It took about five days from Liverpool to Halifax. I was glad to see that the ship didn't have to zigzag for fear of U-boats.

On the way home, all four of us crew members stopped in Montreal to visit Johnny D'Avril's parents. At that time, Johnny was only reported missing. I remember that his father spoke French much better than me.

I had asked Richard Koval to try and find the other three survivors of the *Q Queen*, Flight Sergeant George Tremblay, Flight Sergeant Leo Lamontagne, and Flight Sergeant G. Langevin. Because of their very common French surnames, he was unable to trace Tremblay or Langevin. However, just before I went to visit Joe Parent, I had a call from Richard. He had discovered that Leo Lamontagne's widow, Marjorie, is living in Portage la Prairie, Manitoba. He even had an address and telephone number for her. When I returned from Kapuskasing, I telephoned her.

She was very interested and helpful, but a bit cautious at first. She warned me from the start that she had very little information about her husband's wartime experiences because he had been reluctant to talk about those times. However, after consultation with her daughter, she called me back to tell me what she knew. Later, she also mailed me a large envelope with some documents and photos.

Flight Sergeant Leo Paul Lamontagne, mid-upper gunner of the *Q Queen*, was one of the five men able to bail out of the burning Halifax. Just as Joe Parent and the other two survivors from the plane, he was taken prisoner, held in the Marienberg jail, and then transported to the Moosburg POW camp.

Leo, a farm boy from Saskatchewan, was 19 when he enlisted in 1943. When he bailed out of the burning *Q Queen* and landed in the Ore Mountains with his parachute, he lost one of his boots.

Some of the high-explosive bombs destined for German cities.

He hid for two or three days until he was captured. His widow still has two telegrams that the RCAF sent to his parents in 1945. Both were written in French. In the first telegram, dated March 9, they were told that their son had been reported missing after an overseas air operation on March 6. On May 19, the same office wired that he had arrived in England on May 11. Shortly after his return to England, Leo himself dispatched two telegrams. One was addressed to his mother:

DEAR MOTHER BACK IN ENGLAND EVERYTHING OKAY WILL WRITE SEEING YOU SOON LOVE LEO LAMONTAGNE.

The other, addressed to his fiancée and future wife, was received on May 18, 1945:

REPATRIATED TO ENGLAND MY ADDRESS IS 'LIBER-ATED PRISONER OF WAR RCAF OVERSEAS' AM WELL AND FIT ALL MY LOVE LEO LAMONTAGNE.

Leo Lamontagne told his wife that he had written several letters from the Moosburg POW camp, but they never arrived. The telegrams sent from England were the first indication she and his parents had received that Leo was still alive after being reported missing. Leo died of a heart attack in 1986 at the age of 63.

His widow said that to the end, her husband had some shrapnel in his neck from being grazed by a bullet when he was on a forced march. Leo would never talk to anyone about this injury. Marjorie had always assumed that German soldiers had fired at the prisoners as they were marching, but it is also possible that Leo was wounded when American Thunderbolt aircraft strafed the column of prisoners on April 4, 1945, mistaking them for German soldiers on the march.

"Whenever I asked Leo about the war, he answered, 'You don't want to know.' He just said that he was one of the lucky ones who came home."

Jean-Maurice D'Avril was not one of the lucky ones. Had he been taken to Marienberg to join his fellow crew members, he

Crew of the Q Queen *— Halifax III PN-173, coded KW-Q, March 1945. Back row, left to right: P/O Jean Jacques Desbien (pilot; killed in crash, buried first in Drebach, then in Berlin); F/Sgt G. Tremblay (navigator, POW); F/O Joe Parent, (bomb aimer, POW); F/S Albert Emile Minguet (flight engineer, killed, buried first in Drebach, then in Berlin). Front row, left to right: P/O Jean-Maurice D'Avril (wireless operator/air gunner, POW, murdered in Frankenberg); F/O Leo Lamontagne (mid-upper gunner, POW); F/Sgt G. Langevin (tail gunner, POW).*

might still be alive to tell a tale similar to Joe Parent's. Instead —
for a reason yet unknown — he ended up in Frankenberg where
he met his doom. Why was he isolated from the rest of the crew
after he bailed out? Did he bail out earlier than anyone else and
therefore land farther north than the others? Did his parachute
drift off due to the high wind? Did he walk north after he hit the
ground? Was he the "American" who according to the witness
Elfriede Rupprecht surrendered at the textile mill near Sachsenburg? Sachsenburg, only about five kilometres away from
Frankenberg, is far away from the crash site at Drebach, approximately 30 kilometres to the north. The distance between
Frankenberg and Marienberg is about 26 kilometres. (Both distances are "as the crow flies.") While there is no proof that it was
D'Avril who gave himself up in Sachsenburg, there can be no
doubt that he died in Frankenberg.

CHAPTER 13

Lucky Number:

Parachute 13

Jean-Maurice D'Avril's plane was not the only Canadian bomber to crash in the snow-covered Ore Mountains during the attack on Chemnitz in the late evening of March 5, 1945. A Halifax III from Swordfish Squadron, *NA-204*, coded *6U-J*, piloted by Flight Lieutenant W. (Bill) Mitchell, was also shot down by a German night fighter over Chemnitz. Early in my investigation, I had ruled out the possibility that the Frankenberg murder victim could have come from this bomber because all eight of its crew members were listed as POW. Initially, I had been unable to determine where this plane had crashed. Since all crew members had survived, none of their personnel files were available at Library and Archives Canada, and these records are often the only indication of a crash site. When Joe Parent in Kapuskasing told me that four of his crew had been imprisoned together with five of Mitchell's crew, I contacted Richard Koval again. Would he be able find any of those five men from Swordfish Squadron?

In July 2004, shortly after my call for help, he telephoned and surprised me with the names and telephone numbers of some who are still alive. Seven of the crew had been RCAF, one RAF:

F/Lt W. (Bill) Mitchell (RCAF)
pilot and skipper *(now in Guelph, Ontario)*

F/O R. (Rolly) Barteaux (RCAF)
co-pilot, "second dickie" *(deceased)*

F/Sgt A. (Tommy) Ridley (RAF)
flight engineer *(deceased)*

F/O R. (Doug) Loveridge (RCAF)
navigator *(deceased)*

P/O Frank Mudry (RCAF)
bomb aimer *(now in Swift Current, Saskatchewan)*

P/O W. (Bill) Mosey (RCAF)
wireless operator/air gunner *(now in Chatham, Ontario)*

F/Sgt W. (Bruce) Gill (RCAF)
mid-upper gunner *(now in Whitmore, Alberta)*

P/O John Gendron (RCAF)
tail gunner *(now in Napanee, Ontario)*

I immediately contacted Frank Mudry in Swift Current and Doug Loveridge's widow, Joy Loveridge, in Victoria, B.C. Both told me that Bill Mitchell, the pilot, had appointed tail gunner John Gendron as the official crew historian. They had all deposited their reminiscences with him. Fortunately, John also happened to be closest to me, in Napanee, Ontario. We arranged to meet half-way, in John's birthplace, Smith Falls, Ontario, at the Royal Canadian Legion Hall.

John was only 20 years old in March 1945. He was 80 when we met in August 2004, but he certainly did not look his age. He is physically active and mentally alert, with an excellent memory and a friendly, open disposition. He allowed me to tape our conversation, and I transcribed the story he told me.

Yes, back in 1976, the pilot appointed me crew historian and said: "Find the rest of the crew, and we'll have a reunion." It took me about a year to locate them all. We've had a reunion almost every year since then. Now, there are only five of us alive. We'll have another reunion this October in Victoria.

Chemnitz was the 29th operation for our crew and the 30th for me. It turned out to be our last. Our 415 (Swordfish) Squadron was flying the Halifax III version, which was more powerful than earlier versions, with Hercules engines. The machine we flew on that trip was brand-new, with only 60 hours on it. It took a bomb load of about eight tons. Our base was at Eastmoore. We shared the base with 432 (Leaside) Squadron.

Our bomb aimer, Frank Mudry, had been shot up over Berlin during a previous operation, and his crew had bailed out over Sweden. There, he spent six months in a Swedish

John Gendron in 2004. He was the tail gunner in Halifax III NA-204, coded 6U-J, which also crashed in the Ore Mountains on March 5, 1945.

internment camp before being shipped back to England. Under the Geneva Convention, he was to be sent back to Canada without flying against the enemy again. He wasn't very happy when, in spite of this, he was rerouted to join our squadron as a replacement. He could have been executed if the Germans had found out.

When our squadron took off for Chemnitz, we saw some explosions on the ground in England. Two planes had collided. Of course, we didn't know what was going on. We learned later that some Canadian planes had crashed.

It took us about four hours to fly to Chemnitz. There were over 700 heavy bombers involved. People today can't visualize that happening — 700 bombers! They stretched from one horizon to the other. We were probably on the first wave. When we reached the target area, there were no search lights and no flak around, but there sure were JU 88 night fighters in the air. We had just dropped our bomb load over Chemnitz. The bomb doors were still wide open. The bomb aimer left to take his seat behind the navigator. The pilot had turned 12 degrees to port, when all of a sudden — whoomm! We were hit from below by *schräge Musik*. Because of the sharp turn, the cannon didn't hit us in the middle, but the nose of the plane was completely blown off, and the port wing was on fire. Fire and sparks were going out under my rear turret about eight or nine feet [about three metres], just like a jet. The pilot said: "Hang on! We'll try to make for the Russian lines." We thought they were only about 30 miles [50 kilometres] or so away. But then the pilot said: "I'm losing control. So everybody out! Jump, jump!" It was a miracle that no one was injured or burned. We were all able to bail out.

After our conversation, John sent me an account of a plane going down that night given to him by Charlie Laforce, of

Belleville, Ontario. Charlie had also participated in the big raid on Chemnitz on March 5, 1945, as a wireless operator/air gunner from 424 (Tiger) Squadron. Charlie told John that he witnessed a bomber being attacked and shot down while he was standing behind the mid-upper gunner in the astro dome. He believed this had been Gendron's Halifax III *NA-204*, coded *6U-J*:

What I saw was a Halifax to our port and below us. It was a distance away. A twin-engined aircraft on level flight below the Halifax fired upwards and hit the Halifax, disintegrating the front. The twin-engined could have been a ME 110, but I guessed it to be a JU 88, and since it fired upwards although in level flight, I took it to be *schräge Musik*. A couple of chutes appeared, but I became engaged in watching for fighters, for many were about (to, on, and from the target). It was bright from T.I.s (target indicators), fires, and fighter flares and searchlights … I felt sorry for the "Halley," but I had to watch for fighters and think about our own skins.

John Gendron's own story continues:

Back at the base, when the parachutes were given out, we could pick a number. Of course, we were all superstitious. So I had said: "Give me number 13, it's my lucky number." And they did. And it saved my life.

My chute was in a seat pack, and I kicked myself out. I was one of the first to jump, from 10,000 feet [3,000 metres]. I couldn't say where the others came down, but there might have been a distance of 15 miles [25 kilometres] or more between us. One minute I was way out in the air, five minutes later I was hung up in a tree, about 30 feet [10 metres] from the ground. The top of the chute was caught in this tall fir tree, and I was spinning around, caught in the top of the tree. I couldn't see any of the others, in fact I couldn't see anything. It was dark, and I was in the middle of a snowstorm. It was around 10 in the evening. I sat in the tree for about 10 minutes and noticed that I had no feeling in my left leg. Finally, I used a little knife I had in my pocket to cut the parachute strings. I climbed down and dropped into about three feet of snow. In my survival kit — a plastic box about eight centimetres long — I had a chocolate bar, some gum, a British flag and arm band, a Russian flag and arm band, and a compass. I was thinking of heading east for the Russian lines, or even south all the way to Italy, but I knew it would be impossible to get very far in this deep snow. I followed a road in the forest, which came to a dead end. I followed another, and another. I must have walked around in a circle, floundered is more like it.

Early in the morning I came to a place where they had been cutting wood, and there were two German soldiers who said: "*Hände hoch!*" [Hands up!] I knew a little German and understood what they meant. I raised my arms. They tied my wrists and ankles with rope and took me to the small village of Annaberg where I ended up in a tiny jail.[1] Then they brought in the co-pilot, Rolly Barteaux. This had been his first trip, and I had actually never met him before. The soldiers were pretty good, they first took us to a restaurant to order us a coffee, but everybody there stood up and shouted, "*Terror-flieger!*" They weren't going to let us have anything. So we sort of backed out, and the soldiers took us down to the railway station where we boarded a train for Marienberg. In the jail there, the two of us were put in a cell together with three others from our crew: Bill Mitchell, Doug Loveridge, and Frank Mudry. There were also four French Canadians from the Alouette Squadron (including Joe Parent) and an Australian pilot. There was much surprise when Frank Mudry discovered that his cousin Suzie in Regina was Joe Parent's girlfriend. Joe and Suzie are still married today. Frank was Joe's best man at the wedding. Our pilot had landed only 300 yards [274 metres] from where the plane had crashed. We were still missing Bruce Gill, Tommy Ridley, and Bill Mosey, who had all come down somewhere else.

The 10 of us stayed in Marienberg for about four days. Once every day, they gave us a cup of cold coffee and a piece of black bread. Of course, the German people themselves were in bad shape, too. Finally, they took us to Chemnitz by train. There, we were handed over to our new guards. As we walked through Chemnitz, near the railway station, it was a pretty bad scene, pretty scary. A crowd of perhaps 150 to 200 civilians surrounded us, threatened us. You couldn't blame them because every place was rubble. The same thing would have happened here if we had been bombed the way they were. There was one older gentleman who was very agitated. He held something like a violin case in one hand, and with the other hand he reached across and knocked me flat. He hit me on the side of the head. As I was getting up, I saw the pilot getting knocked down and knocked around. There were 10 German guards, one for each of us, and they had Schmeisser guns. There was a short, older sergeant. He said to us: "If one man escapes, you'll all be shot." We told each other not to try anything. But the German soldiers guarding us saved our lives. They formed a ring around us. I knew enough German to know that they told the people to get back or they would fire. Then a tall German officer came. He was wearing a monocle. He snapped a few orders at the sergeant, and we were taken up to the railway station where there was a brick wall. Here was another crowd including a 14-year-old girl, and she was spitting at us. She was really upset, probably because she had lost someone. The officer told us: "Everybody face the wall!" Then we heard a click ... we thought this was it. But the officer told the girl to get out of there. If the German soldiers hadn't been there, I wouldn't be sitting here, I don't think. Finally, we were loaded onto a train.

It took us two weeks — stop and go — to get to Frankfurt. Somewhere on the way, we were taken to a Luftwaffe
station where we all had our own cell. They fed us big plates
of potatoes and sauerkraut and meat. There was a kind of
rapport between the German Luftwaffe guys and us. From
Frankfurt, we walked for three days to another camp at Wet-
zlar, where the American Red Cross handed out parcels. This
camp was run by American POWs. They gave us soup and
issued us with GI uniforms. Best of all were the boots with
rubber soles, which were much more comfortable to walk
in. I had never seen rubber soles before. Next we were taken
by train, in open box cars, to a camp at Nuremberg, where
we stayed for 10 days. On April 4, we left that camp on foot
at 1 p.m. Fifteen minutes later, 12 American Thunderbolt
fighters strafed us.[2] They thought we were German soldiers
on the move. We all hit for the ditches on both sides of the
road. I heard many of our guys crying for their mother
before they died. On April 24, after a grueling forced march,
we arrived at the big Moosburg POW camp near Munich:
Stalag VII A. There, we were liberated by General Patton's
3rd Army on April 29. The Americans farmed us out
throughout the town of Moosburg to protect German civilians from the Russian prisoners of war, who were on a
rampage after they were set free. Five of us were placed in
the Steinlehner house to protect the older man and woman
and two young girls and a boy who lived there. We were
there for about a week. At 3 a.m. one morning, the woman
in the house next door went hysterical because she thought
that Russians were in her house. Bill Mosey and I rushed
over and slept on the floor with blankets until the morning.

Have you seen the [TV program] called *The Valour and
the Horror* by the McKenna Brothers? There was a whole
bunch of lies in it. They said if we would have known how
many would be killed, we wouldn't fly. We knew how many

would be killed. Sometimes, coming back to base, we had to circle for an hour before landing because they had to unload so many dead and wounded first.

Would we have flown if we would have known we were killing thousands of civilians, would that have made a difference to us? It was a very difficult thing. Magdeburg you could see burn for 100 miles in the air, terrible! It looked like your mother boiling preserves on the stove, all bubbling. You couldn't imagine. We never discussed it much later, back in Canada. We didn't want to talk about the war. Just close the book and try to forget about it.

My efforts to find the exact crash site of Gendron's bomber have not been successful so far. It has to be assumed that the plane came down in the Ore Mountains, reasonably close to the Czech border. The crew members of Halifax III *NA-204*, coded *6U-J*, from 515 (Swordfish) Squadron bailed out near Chemnitz at about the same time as the *Q Queen* crew. The Swordfish crew landed at least 30 kilometres apart from each other. While five of them ended up on the Saxon side of the Ore Mountains in the Annaberg/Marienberg area, the mid-upper gunner and the flight engineer landed south of the border, in a forest on the Czech side of the mountains.

I called the mid-upper gunner, Bruce Gill, in Westlock, Alberta, and he told me his story of that night. After he had parachuted into the snowy forest, he walked until he was spotted and taken into custody by a village blacksmith. After walking for two days, he was transported by bus to a POW camp at Bilin in the Sudetenland (a region of Czechoslovakia under German occupation). There, he met up with one of his crew mates, RAF Flight Sergeant Tommy Ridley, the flight engineer, and the only non-Canadian crew member. Gill had injured his hand upon landing, apparently caught in the parachute strings. At the camp, he was treated by a medical officer from New Zealand. Unfortunately, he later lost a finger due to complications.

When the Red Army occupied the camp in April, Gill heard rumours that all of them — Germans and prisoners alike — were going to be relocated to Russia. Gill decided to try his luck elsewhere. From his crew mates, I heard a most interesting and colourful, albeit second-hand, report about his odyssey. Gill had been a cowboy in Alberta. At the POW camp, he managed to "requisition" a horse. On its back, he make his own way to western Germany, where he was eventually liberated by the Americans. I asked Gill about this story, but unfortunately he was reluctant to talk about it. I have the suspicion that there is enough for a whole other book there.

CHAPTER 14

Drebach

O nce I learned where D'Avril's plane had gone down, I turned again to my cousin Fritz. I asked him to search for witnesses and information on the crash in the villages of Drebach and Herold.

As a native Chemnitzer, Fritz is very familiar with the Ore Mountains, a range whose gradual rise to a height of over 1,000 metres begins in the southern outskirts of the city. What is more, the Chemnitz accent is closely related to the Ore Mountains accent, and strangers who can speak the local lingo are bound to be received more readily than strangers "from away."

Armed with a questionnaire I had prepared for him, Fritz set out for Drebach, which is less than half an hour's drive from Chemnitz. Someone suggested he should talk to one of Drebach's local historians, Kurt Melzer. However, Melzer was in the hospital. His wife suggested Hermann Pährisch, who is very interested in history and genealogy. Pährisch was 14 in 1945. He remembers seeing the wreck of the Canadian bomber a few days after the

Drebach in the Ore Mountains. Photo taken in October 2004 from the site where the Q Queen *crashed on March 5, 1945.*

crash. He and other boys had rummaged through the fuselage, searching for items that boys their age consider useful. I can relate to this because it was on a similar venture that I acquired the flare gun, the "beautiful" weapon I had to surrender when the Americans came to Frankenberg.

Frankenberg, end of April, 1945

I heard that the large army supply depot in nearby Auerswalde had been abandoned by the Wehrmacht and was being looted. People said that it was full of equipment and supplies of all kinds, from bicycles and toothbrushes and chocolate bars to cans of meat and fish to bags of flour. "You can get anything you want by just going there and scooping it up," someone told me. Naturally, I wanted to be there, but my mother and my aunt — the women who controlled my life — didn't want me to go. However, I conspired with my new friend Anneliese Langer, and we both took off on foot. It was an eight-kilometre walk, but easy to find. All we had to do was follow the crowds though the villages of Niederlichtenau and Oberlichtenau.

As we came close to the depot, we met hundreds of people carrying out boxes of food, crates of beer and wine, bags of grain or flour. Many had brought their handcarts and loaded them full of loot: army uniforms, boots, blankets piled high, radios, typewriters, lamps …

The depot was a cavernous building — a giant warehouse. The military, or perhaps the SS, had blown up parts of it, but some sections were still intact. Looking around, we soon realized that the best things had already been taken. Most of what was left consisted of military equipment: gas masks, some ammunition canisters, parts of machine guns, and tires — thousands of tires. Since civilians didn't own cars or trucks, the tires weren't of much use to anyone. Still, people were carting them off. If there was any food left, we didn't see it. But I did spot some things that caught my attention. After all, I was a 13-year-old boy. I grabbed a shiny flare pistol complete with ammunition, a steel helmet, and two beautiful backpacks, into which I stuffed the other items. I also picked up a radio receiver. Anneliese had gathered up similarly "useful" material, and we made our way home. It was slowly getting dark. I was very proud of my new possessions, but when I showed them to the women at home, they were not pleased. Not only had I disobeyed them, they said, but I had also brought "completely useless items."

"Why didn't you bring any food? Or uniform coats? Or blankets? What are you going to do with this ridiculous junk?"

I was disappointed and now angry at myself. What had possessed me to take only these army things? They no longer seemed important to me now. I took the army backpacks to our attic room and stashed everything under my cot. The next day, someone said that if the Bolsheviks came, they would immediately shoot anyone in possession of Nazi or army items. We should destroy or hide everything that might stamp us as Nazis. A few days later, I buried my prized flare gun with its ammunition in the garden behind the house, along with other "contraband."

Pährisch told Fritz that another local man, Kurt Scheffler, could probably be of help as well. Fritz found Scheffler in the neighbouring hamlet of Venusberg. His recollections matched those of Hermann Pährisch. For several years, Scheffler had been in charge of the motorcycle museum in the nearby castle of Augustusburg. This museum is located very close to the town of Zschopau where the famous DKW motorcycles were built. The factory was founded in 1906 by the Danish entrepreneur Jorge Skafte Rasmussen, who had studied engineering in Chemnitz. After World War II, Zschopau continued to produce motorcycles under the name of MZ (Motor Works Zschopau). In 1945, going through the wreckage of the crashed Canadian Halifax, young Scheffler had spotted a small motorcycle or scooter-like vehicle that was damaged beyond repair. However, he took out the small vehicle's gasoline motor, which was more or less intact. He later restored the "looted" motor and donated it to the museum in Augustusburg, where it can be seen today.

This find presents a bit of a mystery. How did a small motorcycle get into a Halifax on a bomber mission over Germany? The name plate on the motor shows a large letter *M* and the inscription "8th S.G.D.G." There is a possibility that the motor came from a Corgi, a British-built mini-motorcycle whose wheels were only 25 centimetres in diameter. It was a common means of transportation at Bomber Command air bases in Yorkshire. Did one of the crew members use it to drive out to the runway and then clandestinely stow it on board? This is what Bill Tytula of the Halifax Project at the RCAF Museum in Trenton suggests. He says people called these mini-bikes "line vehicles." The museum staff in Augustusburg would also like to know more about the origin of the motorcycle and why it was on board this plane.

I questioned Joe Parent, John Gendron, and several other veterans of Bomber Command about this motorcycle and its surviving motor. While Joe feels it would have been impossible to stow it inside the Halifax, John thinks it might have worked. John also confirmed that the little Corgis were very popular at the British bases.

Both Pährisch and Scheffler clearly remember the exact site where the Halifax crashed late in the evening of March 5, 1945. Earlier, the plane must have lost two engines and possibly a whole wing, because only the fuselage and two engines were found at the main crash site along a stretch of road known locally as *Langes Gewende* (the long turn). Other small parts of the plane were scattered over an area of about 500 metres on both sides of this road.

The only industry in Drebach during the war was a former stocking factory that had been retooled to produce altimeters for Junkers aircraft. Perhaps because of this, the village was bombed on February 14, 1945. A few houses and barns were destroyed and several people were killed, but the factory survived intact and stood until it was demolished in 2002.

Scheffler told Fritz that one engine from the Halifax had been lowered into one of the craters left by the earlier bombing, while the fuselage and the other engine were pulled to a gully near the village and then buried.

Years after the crash, people tried to find the engines with metal detectors, but to no avail. Scheffler said that there could be some local residents or their descendants who are in possession of small fragments of the crashed plane. However, the only piece of material that he can trace with certainty to the Halifax III *PN-173*, coded *KW-Q*, is the gasoline motor in Augustusburg.

Fritz also sent me copies of some documents now in the Marienberg District Archives. They demonstrate that the local authorities responded correctly and honourably to the tragedy in their small town. On March 7, 1945, Mayor Ossmann of Drebach wrote to the military commander in Marienberg: "Enclosed please find the papers found on board the four-engine English [*sic*] bomber which crashed in the local area at about 11 p.m. on March 5, 1945."

A receipt issued on the same day by the Wehrmacht commander in Marienberg acknowledges that the following items were turned over by the municipal authorities in Drebach: one navigator's log book with seven handwritten pages, one linen satchel with fourteen maps, four routing lists, seven loose maps. On March 10, the Mayor again wrote to Marienberg, reporting that the bodies of two Canadian airmen were found in the wreckage of the bomber. The report listed the names, ranks, and serial numbers of Jean Jacques Desbien and Albert Emile Minguet. The bodies had been taken to the local morgue. All items found on the bodies were secured and listed in detail by *Heimbürgerin* Olga Loos, who was paid 8.50 *reichsmark* for the four hours it had taken her.[1] On March 11, 1945, the two Canadians were buried at the Drebach cemetery.

In October 2004, I decided to return to Germany. My investigation still had too many important "missing links," and I couldn't expect others to do all the work for me. For a few days, I stayed with Fritz and his wife, Irmgard, in Chemnitz. Then I drove up into the mountains, to Drebach.

I had been all over the Ore Mountains before, as a child, and on several holidays. Among my favourite places are Seiffen, where dozens of carvers and turners produce handmade Christmas decorations and toys; Olbernhau, the town where the Christmas nutcracker originated; and Annaberg, once a famous silver mining town.

The Ore Mountains are my favourite part of Germany, and I have some deep ancestral roots there. The mountains offer few spectacular sights. The scenery is mostly pleasant in a quiet way, with rather poor farmland, deep coniferous forests, broad valleys, and mountain-top lookouts. The people of the region are shaped by the land. Typically, they are down-to-earth, modest, honest, and friendly. Music plays a major role in their lives.

But I had never been to Drebach. I heard the name for the first time when I learned that Jean-Maurice D'Avril's Halifax had crashed there.

I had already called Hermann Pährisch from Canada to arrange a meeting. Pährisch in turn had contacted three other men who also remembered the crash of the Canadian bomber. They all live in the village, and they were all gathered at Pährisch's home when I arrived. Although born in Drebach, Pährisch and his family had been living in Chemnitz in 1945. However, on March 5, when Chemnitz was attacked, he happened to be visiting his grandmother in Drebach. Although he didn't see or hear the plane coming down, since it occurred near the other end of the long village, he remembers being told about the crash the next morning. On March 6, he went back home to Chemnitz.

My father was away as a soldier, and I wanted to see whether my mother was all right after the attack. I walked from Drebach to Thum. From there, I took a bus into the burning city of Chemnitz. I will never forget walking home along Fürstenstrasse, near the Humboldthöhe. It was there when for the first time in my life I saw a dead body. As I came close to the Findeisen factory yard, I saw a corpse which was lying behind a fence, face down. I remember that all the outer clothes were gone, and I saw nothing but bluish underwear. Someone told me that he had been an enemy airman, and that everything else — his overalls, uniform, boots, and watch — had been stolen by looters.

Sitting on a large sofa in the Pährisch living room were the three Drebach neighbours, Achim Hartmann, Manfred Heeg, and Lothar Ficker, who had seen and heard the Canadian bomber flying very low over their houses before it crashed. They all told me about the plane flying low above the rooftops, with its engines and wings on fire. They remembered the tremendous crash. They recalled going out to see parts of the wreckage in the morning.

This is how Achim Hartmann recalls the night of March 5, 1945:

There was a huge commotion outside, plane noises. It actually sounded like several planes right above us, and there were probably fighters as well. Our window was facing out back, in the direction of the plane crash. My mother said to me: "Look, there is something burning out there!" But we didn't dare go outside. We were glad that everything seemed to be over. And then on the next day, we could see what had happened, that a plane had crashed. We weren't allowed to go out directly to the crash site. It was cordoned off, and some flak soldiers [anti-aircraft gunners] were posted as guards. They had pulled some kind of tape all around. The guards stayed at the fuselage until the two bodies were taken away.[2] After that, it wasn't as strictly guarded.

An incredible amount of snow had fallen that night, a regular snowstorm. The more courageous people went out to see the wreckage, and they had already formed a narrow path in the deep snow, leading out to the wreckage. We still weren't allowed to get very close. But only 100 or 200 metres from our houses, we spotted an engine that was partly buried in the ground, and about 200 metres further on, just in front of a little woods, the undercarriage had hit the ground. It stayed there for many years.

Drebach in the winter.

The fuselage itself was on the other side of the little woods, where the big beech tree is still standing. The plane had cleared the trees and crashed immediately behind them, in a snow-covered field. Later, we boys went exploring inside the fuselage. There was a lot of felt around the tanks, felt in blue and white layers, at least two centimetres thick. Manfred Heeg took it out, and the shoemaker made soles for slippers out of the felt. For the longest time, a large piece of this felt was still lying around, showing all the outlines of the soles which the shoemaker had cut out. He had given us the rest. Too bad, we didn't keep it. Someone had also cut the tires off the landing gear and recycled the rubber. We were all too young to know how to utilize things from the plane, but the adults dismantled and salvaged all kinds of useful objects, such as many electrical parts and devices. The plane was full of electrical equipment. After some of the fuselage had already been dragged away, I unscrewed a high-speed electrical motor from its bracket in what remained of the wreckage. I think it was in the radio operator's console, in the mid-section of the fuselage, behind the cockpit. Much later — I think just last year — I gave it to Arnold Dirk who lives in the lower part of the village. We also dismantled pieces of Plexiglas from around the cockpit, and took them home.

It's a pity that nothing is left, not the felt or anything. For many years, I still had a large piece of rounded sheet metal from the plane. We used it as a cover to keep stacks of firewood dry when it rained. It had several reinforcement ribs on the inside. I only gave it away two or three years ago as scrap metal.

Hermann Pährisch remembers that the fuselage was dragged away from the crash site in pieces and dropped into a nearby gully.[3] He explained that there were two roads in that area, one higher up and one low down. That is where the fuselage was left, together with one of the engines and many other parts of the wreck.

Pährisch continued:

Shortly after the war, I worked for a man called Hans Weiss, who had started a shop producing folk art.[4] He wanted to make a fancy sign with the firm name on it, *Drebacher Kunstwerkstatt — DKW*. He sent me out to the wreck with a hammer and chisel to cut a large piece of metal from the fuselage, and the sign was made from this. Later, Weiss went bankrupt and moved away, to Cologne. The house was sold, and I don't know whether that sign is still there or not. The gully, into which the wreckage had been dropped, later served as a garbage dump for a while, and it was covered up with earth. Later, a hog farm was established on the site, and some of it may actually cover the exact spot where the wreckage was buried.

Manfred Heeg said:

There can be no justification for crimes like the murder of the Canadian airman in Frankenberg by people who were fanatics. But on the other hand … for example, there was a young woman who lived in Achim Hartmann's house, Trautel Helwig. She was only in her early twenties. She and some others went out with a team of horses in the direction of Scharfenstein, to bring firewood from the forest. Achim and I remember it very well. We were just coming home from school because there was an air-raid alert. Suddenly an airplane appeared, swooping down very low over the roofs of our houses, and fired at the horse-drawn vehicle, which certainly had nothing to do with the war effort. One of the horses was killed. Trautel was seriously injured and soon died. There is no justification for that either, and I think we still haven't learned from that.

While Frau Pährisch was serving coffee and *Pfefferkuchen* (gingerbread) cookies, I learned from the men that a German fighter aircraft had also crashed near Drebach late at night on March 5, 1945. Heeg and Hartmann had heard machine gun fire overhead. They now speculated whether the gunners in the Canadian bomber might have hit the fighter before bailing out. It could even have been the same Focke Wulff 190 that had attacked the bomber. They also remembered that several parachutes were found in the wreckage of the Halifax. Later, the women and girls of the village used the fine silk from the parachutes to make dresses and blouses. Immediately after the end of the war, when all food was extremely scarce, this parachute fabric also became a coveted commodity in an economy that ran primarily on bartering. The villagers took pieces of silk to the farmers and traded them for food.

Lothar Ficker vividly remembers the Canadian airman (probably Leo Lamontagne) who was taken prisoner the morning after the crash:

They came to our door, the airman and a German who was guarding him. Some other boys and I were standing around. The guard asked Gerhard Wenzel, the village's fire chief and air-raid warden, to telephone the authorities. The Canadian kept saying "*Polizei, Polizei.*" It seemed to be the only German word he knew. We thought that these airmen might have been told to report to the police in case they were ever shot down, and that this man now wanted to be handed over to the police. I remember that the Canadian airman was quite tall. He had black hair and was not wearing a hat. That was the last I ever heard about this affair.

We all drove a short distance to look at the crash site, just outside Drebach. Near the small woods called *Rüdiger Busch*, close to where the landing gear had come down, stood a bench where hikers could rest. We talked to some people who had stopped at this bench. To my surprise, one of them, Eberhard Gerlach, also remembered the crash of March 5, 1945. Not only did he remember it, but he, too, had crawled into the fuselage after the guard was withdrawn. I was thrilled when he told me that he still had a steel bolt, more than an inch (about three centimetres) in diameter, four inches (10 centimetres) long, including a thick base plate and a thread with a pin hole for a cotter pin at the top. Gerlach had taken it from the landing gear of the Halifax and kept it all these years. He was kind enough to part with it. He gave it to me when I told him that it was perhaps the only surviving physical remnant of the *Q Queen*.[5] I was very grateful for Gerlach's generosity. He told me that he had treasured the bolt all his life as a memento of World War II and his childhood.

"But after what you told me about the young Canadian airman who was murdered, I want you to have it and take it back to Canada. I think it will be better in Canada than here, where it would be discarded one day as a meaningless piece of junk after I'm gone." I brought it with me, and I may eventually donate this prized possession to a museum.

Two other artifacts have been located in Drebach since I was there last. They are two "steady bushings" (support bushings) for the control tube that linked the pilot's controls to the wings and the tail. One of these still contains a swivel bearing with 40 steel balls. The supports are made of a phenolic material, an early form of plastic, and are about 54 millimetres high and 61 millimetres wide. These pieces were removed from the tail of the crashed Halifax by Gottfried Wolff (now of Gelenau), who lived in Drebach in 1945 as a 14-year-old boy. He also removed the wireless operator's Marconi radio set, which he kept for many years. He says that in this particular version, only six of its potential ten tubes had been inserted. Unfortunately, Wolff disposed of the radio a few years ago. He also remembers finding a first-aid kit and flares of several colours.

Eyewitnesses to the crash in Drebach. Left to right: Achim Hartmann, Manfred Heeg, Eberhard Gerlach, Hermann Pährisch, Lothar Ficker. Photo taken in October 2004.

There are now four surviving artifacts of the *Q Queen*: the steel bolt, the mysterious motorcycle motor (in the Augustusburg museum), and the two support bushings.

Eberhard Gerlach told me how excited he had been as a boy about the crash, this big event which had brought the war so close to their little mountain village. In the morning after the crash, he first went to inspect the landing gear, one of the engines, and the huge propeller blades, which he initially thought were the wings of the plane. Then he walked around the woods to see the big fuselage,

marvelling at its size. Until then, the only planes he had ever seen were the British and American formations flying high overhead to attack industrial targets in Bohemia across the nearby border. He also remembers that one of the enormous wings of the Halifax was on the snow-covered ground. Ammunition was strewn all over inside the wreck. He will never forget seeing the bodies of

Support bushing pulled from the tail of the Halifax III which crashed at Drebach.

the two Canadian airmen still inside the fuselage. He was horrified to see that one of the heads had lost its skull cap. Gerlach remembers that there were two Canadian prisoners [most likely Leo Lamontagne and Joe Parent] in the village that morning. His sister had told him that she had been at the municipal office where she saw two "enemy airmen."

Then Gerlach suggested I should go and see someone else in the village, Egon Lötzsch, who might know something about the incident. I met Lötzsch and his wife outside their son's home. They already knew from the newspaper reports that I would visit the village to ask questions about the Canadian bomber. Lötzsch said he would be glad to talk to me.

> I was 14 at the time of the crash. I heard the bomber come overhead late in the night. I noticed that the plane seemed to be pursued by a German night fighter, a Messerschmitt 110. The fighter also crashed not far away from here, in An der Laube, a forest between Drebach and Hopfgarten. I went to see that wreckage too. I know that in the same night, some Canadian airmen had parachuted to safety in the Hopfgarten area.

Local historian Fritz Uhlig of Hopfgarten knows the exact location where the German fighter crashed, but has been unable to establish the identity of the pilot. One of the Canadians may have been Flying Officer Joe Parent, the bomb aimer, who was taken prisoner in the early morning, after spending the night hidden in the woods.

Lötzsch and another boy had gone to see the wreckage in the morning. They found that the fuselage had broken in half, which could mean that the pilot may have attempted a belly landing. The tail and the rear section of the fuselage, including the rear gunner's pod, were lying in one place, and the main part of the fuselage in another. It had one of the wings attached, but without the engines.

I saw the two dead airmen, in their brown overalls, on the ground, near the tail section and not near the front of the plane. One of the dead had a smashed skull. It was the first time I ever saw a human brain.

Lötzsch remembers that he did not smell any fuel as he entered the fuselage from the rear and that he crawled all the way through to the front section. The fuselage was not burned out, but more or less intact, except that the outside was buckled.

There was one thing that really surprised me — I have told this to many people. Here, in the mountain villages, our normal toilets consisted of primitive outhouses. In the bomber, we found a real flush toilet, with linoleum all around.

Lötzsch also told me that he found the cockpit of the plane completely intact. This observation is puzzling, since he saw the two dead — the pilot and the flight engineer — lying on the ground near the tail of the plane, about 10 or 15 metres away from the fuselage.

I learned from Lötzsch that the woman who first encountered the

Canadian airman (probably Leo Lamontagne) as he walked toward the village, was Sister Klara, the village's nursing sister, who wore a large, white-winged cap.

She accompanied this man to the church. He was limping. [Leo Lamontagne had lost one boot.] She made him sit down on the steps and wait. My father, Walter Lötzsch, was the owner and operator of a bus. He regularly drove

Left to right: Egon Lötzsch, Hermann Pährisch. October 2004.

the workers from the village to the factory early in the morning. He was told to load the Canadian airman in his bus and drop him off at the municipal office, which is about two kilometres from the church. There was a small cell behind the office. There, a second Canadian airman had already shown up who had surrendered in another part of the village [most likely Flying Officer Joe Parent]. The next day, after Gerhard Wenzel had telephoned the authorities, Albin Günther came with a horse-drawn sleigh. He was ordered to take the prisoners to Marienberg.

Joe Parent remembers a sleigh ride, but thinks that he was the only prisoner in the sleigh, and that in addition to the driver, there was only one German who guarded him and held a pistol to his head. It is therefore likely that Lamontagne and Parent were taken to Marienberg separately.

The Germans buried Desbien and Minguet in the village cemetery, in the presence of the Mayor, the Police Chief, and a Wehrmacht corporal from Marienberg. In the summer of 1945, after the war had ended, some British soldiers came to Drebach in army vehicles, exhumed the bodies, and took them away. They were moved to the Allied War Cemetery in Berlin, where Jean-Maurice D'Avril was ultimately buried as well.

CHAPTER 15

Next of Kin

On August 3, 2004, my wife, Elizabeth, and I drove to Montreal. From Jean-Maurice D'Avril's personnel file, I knew that in 1945, his family had lived at 4603 Rue Chabot. My goal was to discover whether any relatives of the "unknown Canadian" were still alive. I knew his parents were Henri D'Avril and Cecile, née Duffy, but I assumed that they were no longer living, since they would have to be close to 100 years old. I also knew that there had been a younger sister, Lise. However, since most women changed their surnames when they married, until recently, I was not very hopeful that I would be able to find her.

From the Autoroute, I took the Papineau exit to St-Joseph. We stopped for a coffee before proceeding to Rue Chabot. Looking around, I noticed the faces of many ethnic minorities and wondered how much the D'Avril neighbourhood might have changed in almost 60 years. Would I find the house at all or a new apartment block in its place? Would the occupants of the house — if it

Where Jean-Maurice D'Avril grew up: 4603 Rue Chabot in Montreal. Photo taken in 2004.

was still there — be recent arrivals to the city with no memory of Montreal in World War II? As we drove south on Rue Chabot, my hopes went up: in most blocks, the old rows of houses were still intact, complete with their ornamental iron stairways, which are character-istic of Montreal.

We found number 4603 and parked across the street. A light rain had begun to fall. Elizabeth waited in the car. I walked to the front door and saw that the house had two numbers, one for downstairs and one for upstairs. The upstairs was 4603. I rang the doorbell in anticipation. Soon an elderly gen-tleman came down the stairs. I introduced myself and greeted him in my rudimentary French. To my relief, he invited me to speak English. His name was Fernand Lessard. Yes, he remembered the D'Avril family very well. He used to live across the street. His father owned the house where the D'Avrils were tenants. Since they moved out in the 1950s, Mon-sieur Lessard and his wife have been living in the apartment they used to occupy. Yes, of course, he remembered Jean-Maurice — a very nice, good-looking, tall, soft-spoken young man, a few years older than he himself. He, Lessard, had only been 17 in 1945, and thus he had just missed the military draft. He remembered how devastated the D'Avril family had been when their only son was first reported missing — so close to the end of the war — and when he was later presumed dead. Lessard thought that the par-ents never really believed that Jean-Maurice was dead. "They were hoping till the very end he would return some day." Lessard didn't know that Jean-Maurice's body was identified and buried in Berlin in 1948. By that time, Henri and Cecile D'Avril had moved away. Lessard told me that the parents had died a long time ago. Yes, he knew that there was a daughter, Lise, a little girl a lot younger than her brother. He had also heard that she was married, but had no idea what her married name was or where she was living.

Monsieur Lessard asked me to come upstairs and introduced me to his wife. I already knew what schools Jean-Maurice had attended and in what church the family had worshipped. The Lessards told me how to find them, just a few blocks away. Then Monsieur Lessard offered a parting bit of advice: "You should go and see Richard Lemerise on Bordeaux Street. He used to live next door. He just might remember Lise's married name."

I took some photos of the house and the street where Jean-Maurice spent his childhood and early youth. In pouring rain, we drove to find the Lemerise residence. There was no one at home. We then paid a visit to the parish office of the family's church, St-Pierre Claver Church, a massive neo-Romanesque stone structure on St-Joseph Boulevard. The secretary was neither very interested, nor helpful. No documents or records pertaining to the D'Avril family could be produced. I did take some photos of the church,

On the steps of Ecole St-Pierre-Claver in Montreal, about 1936. Jean-Maurice is in the back row, first from the left.

of D'Avril's elementary school, the Ecole St-Pierre-Claver, and of his high school, the Ecole Supérieure St-Stanislas.

Twice we tried the house on Bordeaux Street again, to no avail. I finally left a note with my name and telephone number and explained what I was looking for. The trip to Montreal had been partly successful, but I still did not know Lise's last name or whereabouts.

Over the next two days, I tried to call the Lemerise family and left several messages on their answering machine. Finally Mme Lemerise called me back, only to disappoint me. No, neither she nor her husband were able to help me. They did not know Lise's name or where she lived.

Before going to Montreal, I had already contacted the only two D'Avrils in the city's telephone directory. The subscribers could not help me and apparently had no connection with the family of Jean-Maurice. I then went on the Internet and found two other people in Montreal with the rare name of D'Avril. Their name had not appeared in the telephone directory. I sent them an e-mail, asking them for information. In the evening, just after we had returned from Montreal, I received a telephone call from a man named Alain D'Avril. He had never heard the name of Jean-Maurice, Henri, or Lise D'Avril, but he was going to ask his mother and get back to me. The next day, April 4, I received the following e-mail message:

Hi Mr. Hessel, I have a phone number for you, she's a sister of Jean-Maurice D'Avril: Lise D'Avril Desjardins (514) … Good luck! Alain D'Avril.

Good luck indeed! I immediately called Lise in Montreal. I was very excited, but also apprehensive. How would I handle this conversation, and probably in French to boot? I didn't know what to expect. How would Jean-Maurice's sister react to my news? How should I tell her about her brother? I wanted to be careful not to upset her or interfere with her perception of his death. I knew that the parents had been notified first of his "presumed death" and then of his actual death after the grave was found in Berlin. So Lise would have been told that, but not the manner of his death.

When I heard her voice, I apologized for my bad French and asked hopefully whether she spoke any English. I was greatly relieved to find that her English is very good. She used to work for the federal government, the Department of Public Works, at a time when English was almost the only language in the public service, even for those working in Montreal. It would have been extremely difficult for me to express myself adequately in French, especially in such a delicate matter. I soon discovered that my worries were unfounded. Lise told me immediately that she wanted to know everything, regardless of the circumstances. She had always been puzzled over her brother's fate. "I want to know the truth," she said.

Henri D'Avril married Cecile Duffy, of St-Calixte, Quebec, on June 20, 1921. Their only son, Henri Jean-Maurice Joseph, was born in February 1923. Their only daughter, Lise, was born almost 15 years later, in 1937. Even though Lise was only six years old when

Jean-Maurice and Lise D'Avril in 1944.

her brother was first reported missing in 1945, she still remembers her shock and her parents' despair. She also remembers when Joe Parent and the other surviving crew members of Jean-Maurice's bomber came to visit right after the war. At that time, no one knew what had happened to the missing airman. Even after her parents had received the Certificate of Presumption of Death, they were still hoping that he was suffering from amnesia and would be coming home one day, just like so many other young Canadians. She recalls that the family was later told that her brother's grave had been found in Berlin, and that most likely his parachute had failed to open after his plane was hit during the operation against Chemnitz. Lise did not remember ever hearing of Frankenberg, although the RCAF had advised her parents in 1949 that that was where his grave had been found.

It was a very emotional experience for me to tell Lise about the murder of her brother. After her initial amazement and surprise,

Jean-Maurice's crests and medals: Lise's cherished mementos of her brother.

she asked many questions, and I gave her the answers I knew. I told her that he bailed out and was taken prisoner, that he must have spent some time in custody as a prisoner of war, before he was walked to the railway station in Frankenberg and ambushed. I told her that I had learned much, but that there were still some puzzles, and that the precise date of death was still unknown. Jean-Maurice's date of death was officially set at March 5, 1945. This would have been accurate, had he indeed died as a result of the crash. But of course, he did not.

Lise told me that her parents are both dead. Her mother, Cecile, died in 1969 at the age of 69, and her father, Henri, died in 1988 at the age of 89. But she had many photos of her brother and other relevant documents that were left to her by her parents. She also confirmed what Joe Parent had already told me in Kapuskasing, that Jean-Maurice had been engaged to a girl called Margot Chayer.[1] Lise and I agreed to meet as soon as possible to exchange information.

After an intensive search of seven months, I had reached another of my main objectives: I had located close relatives of the "unknown Canadian airman." I was particularly satisfied that Lise was happy, grateful, and eager to learn more.

On September 17, 2004, Lise and her son, Jean Desjardins, came to visit and spent a day with us. They brought with them several photo albums, letters, and other documents, as well as Jean-Maurice's RCAF crests and medals. Jean Desjardins's face has a striking, almost eerie resemblance to that of his uncle Jean-Maurice D'Avril. Judging by the many photos spread out on our kitchen table, he is also of the same height and build.

There are many photos from

Jean-Maurice D'Avril (middle) in 1935 as a 12-year old Cub Scout.

Jean-Maurice's days as a Cub Scout and later as a Boy Scout. The Cub Scout photos of 1935 remind me of my time in the Hitler Youth. I have only one photo of myself in Jungvolk uniform, taken in January 1944. Comparing these pictures, it occurred to me that we had a few things in common. We both wore uniforms: shorts, shirt with but-ton-flap pockets, neckerchief. We both carried pennants. Both Jean-Maurice and I had dark wavy hair. But that's where the similarity ends.

The author, 12 years old, in Hitler Youth (Jungvolk) uniform, January 1944.

In the Hitler Youth, we were clev-erly and systematically indoctrinated in Nazi ideology including racism, especially anti-semitism, the concepts of "racial superiority" and "racial hygiene," nationalistic chauvinism, fanatical intolerance to everything and everyone considered "abnormal," and, of course, the absolute worship of Adolf Hitler. It was drilled into us that blind obedience and total subordination to our leaders were great virtues. The individual counted for nothing, was as a bee in a beehive. The whole — the German people, the Nazi movement, the glory of the Third Reich — was all that counted. Had I been old enough, I would have been eager to fight alongside everyone else.

Certainly as a Cub Scout, Jean-Maurice also had to conform to rules of behaviour and perhaps even doctrines. But he was allowed and encouraged to retain and develop his own personality, his likes and dislikes. The Scout movement does not produce robots.

The day when Lise and Jean Desjardins came to visit was not long enough. We had so much to tell each other. They trusted me with their precious photo albums, documents, medals, crests, and, of course, the diary. They left these treasures with me for photocopying and identification. When we said goodbye, we parted like old friends who had much in common. Two days later, I was happy to receive an e-mail from Jean:

Lise and Jean Desjardins meet the author at his home in Waba, September 2004.

The day we spent at your place was not an ordinary day for my mother and me. As we came back, our heads where filled with questions about war(s), and filled with images about the murder of Jean-Maurice. It was not very easy. I believe a book like yours will be good for future generations. They have to know what happened.

– Jean Desjardins,
September 19, 2004

Jean-Maurice D'Avril as RCAF Flight Sergeant, 1944.

These two portraits of Jean-Maurice D'Avril were taken in the studio of Photo Allard of Montreal, perhaps both at about the same time in 1944, shortly before his embarkation for Britain.

On the back of the portrait depicting him in uniform, Jean-Maurice wrote (in French):

I don't know if my premonition will come true. I hope with all my heart it will not. But when I saw this portrait, it seemed that it was shrouded in clouds. I am also telling Margot that I don't like this portrait. It is a good likeness, but to me, it is symbolic. I hope and pray to the Sacred Heart of Jesus and Mary that it will prove me wrong.

Studio portrait of Jean-Maurice D'Avril, 1944.

CHAPTER 16

Mon Journal Outre-mer

Perhaps the greatest treasure Lise Desjardins left with me the day she and Jean visited us in Waba was the diary that was returned to Jean-Maurice's father in 1946. It is a simple black notebook. Jean-Maurice called it *Mon Journal Outre-mer* (My Overseas Journal). As Lise carefully and thoughtfully handed it to me, I had a vision of the young man bending over it, perhaps sitting on his bunk or at a small table under a dim light bulb in his hut at the training camp for wireless operators. What an experience to hold this treasure in my hands. My heart beat faster at the opportunity to read some of the sentiments he expressed. However, to my great disappointment, I found that someone, likely the RAF or RCAF censor in Britain, had torn out all the pages following May 26, 1944. Regrettably, no one will ever know what thoughts he may have recorded in the days and weeks before his last flight.

The diary begins with an account of his crossing, "*Résumé de la Traversie.*" After leaving the training facility in Lachine, he was able to go to Montreal by car. There, he took tearful leave of his fiancée, Margot (*ma Margotton*), her mother, and his parents. They would never see him again.

> It was difficult to see all of them, their eyes full of water, and most of all, my little fiancée. My goodness, she was beautiful in her special dress ... and if I had listened to myself, I would still be with her today ... With a heavy heart, I took a last look around, seeing my Margot shaking with tears ...

At 8 a.m. on March 20, 1944 he left Montreal by train for Halifax.

> As the train moved farther and farther away from Montreal, I took a last look around, thinking of the time when I will return, a time to which I am looking forward so much ...

After having spent two days and two nights on the train, he had "a good but exhausting train ride." He found the very narrow, hard benches of the railway car not very comfortable for sleeping. The train arrived at the railway station in Halifax in the morning of March 22. He was directed to the YMCA where he had lunch and "a great shower. I really needed one."

Eventually, he and his comrades were taken to the docks to board their vessel, the 46,000 ton *Nieuw Amsterdam*. This huge Dutch cruise ship, which was launched as a "floating palace" in 1938, had been seized and pressed into war service by the British who converted

Jean-Maurice with his fiancée, Margot Chayer. Montreal, early 1944.

Jean-Maurice (middle) and two of his fellow airmen in England.

it into a troop carrier with a capacity of 10,000 troops.[1]

... after leaving the port of Halifax on a beautiful Sunday morning at 8:30, the 26th of March, we were all on the bridge. I took one last look, thinking of the day when we would finally return from the war.

The crossing really was very quiet, with nothing abnormal happening, except for a submarine that was spotted about 10 miles ahead of the ship. I had to stand guard on the ship with another 20 men. We worked four hours and then took eight hours off. The food was awful, and there were bugs in it. As a result, we ate only bread and butter.[2]

After six days on the high sea, with no one really being seasick, we finally saw land on Saturday morning, April 1st. It was beautiful, but not like the land in Canada.

At about 7:30 in the evening, the ship entered "*une baie*" (the Firth of Clyde) which leads to Greenock, Scotland. Soon, the airmen destined for service in Bomber Command were taken ashore in a small vessel. At the docks in Greenock Harbour, they walked to a waiting train.

There, on the train, they had installed tables where girls served us a warm meal, tea, and doughnuts. My first impression, when I saw the trains, was that they were sort of comical because they were so small.

Then followed a 17-hour train ride south through England, during which they passed "towns and villages, bridges and tunnels." Jean-Maurice found the trip tiring because "there was hardly any space," and also because "it wasn't smelling very good." They arrived at Bournemouth, the seaside resort on the English Channel, at four in the afternoon on Sunday, April 2.

> There, it was funny to see people looking out of their windows to see "us guys" passing by. The town is really very pretty, and one wouldn't know that this country is at war … After our supper, and after we had settled in our rooms, we took a little walk just to familiarize ourselves with the old town. What struck us the most was the buses that were piled one on top of the other. Also we found that the cars are driving differently than in Montreal, on the other side of the road.

Most of all, he was quite confused with "the famous English money with its shillings and pounds, etc." Easter Sunday was on April 9. He found it very hard to spend this day so far away from home and his fiancée.

Jean-Maurice's account of the voyage and the first few days in England is followed by daily entries from April 12 to May 25, 1944. All these diary pages were written when he was still enrolled in the training program at Bournemouth and at the 3rd RCAF Personnel Recruitment Centre in Staverton, Gloucestershire. More than six months would pass before he was to join the Alouette Squadron at Tholthorpe, Yorkshire. From here on, I will let the diary speak for itself.

> **Wednesday, April 12:** a wonderful day. There was nothing to do in the morning and again nothing to do in the afternoon. So we went to get some rackets at the Knights of Columbus and played tennis at Meyrick Park, a beautiful place. And we're going to go back again.

Thursday, April 13: again nothing much to do except to go to the movies … I also had a little bit of the blues, and for the first time, I got to write to *ma pitoune* [sweetheart].

On Friday, before lunch, we had "clothing parade." We got all our equipment for flying, oxygen masks, etc., a lot of "stuff." In the afternoon, I had nothing to do, so I wrote to Margot, stayed in my room and went to bed at a good time. It was a good day, and two good first weeks. I hope it will always be like this. I hope not to stay here too long. It isn't too bad. We're fed well, and I have a good bed, good pastimes and of course good friends.

April 15, 1944: Today is a big day because it's the third anniversary of Margot and me. Three years that we're going out together. Boy, that was beautiful, but also it was short. And mostly, I regret nothing, and never will I leave her again. I hope it's the last time we celebrate apart from each other … because it's really difficult, and I'm terribly bored. All day my thoughts are with her, *ma pitoune*, of the first days we went out together, our outings, our first kisses, our love and our engagement, etc. … like the promise to abstain from chocolate, just till I return. I will always remain your Jean to you, only to my Margot, that's a promise. You know what I mean …

At two in the afternoon, there was a parade, and there was a draft, but I wasn't on it, I was happy to be dismissed … It was raining, and the temperature was really horrible.

In the evening, I went back to   *"Ma Margotton, ma pitoune …"*

the movies with the gang. We saw *Our West, Seven Sinners* and *The House of Seven Gables*. It wasn't so bad. At the beginning, it was pretty tough and boring. After that, I went to eat at the Knights of Columbus.

In one word, today was a good day, and I remain to you *le même Jean, Jeantin* to you alone, *ma Margotton*. Bye, *ma pitoune*.

April 16, 1944: … At 9 o'clock to the parade. There, we did nothing, only answered to the roll call, and then we were dismissed. Since it was too late to go to the 9:15 mass, I returned to my room and waited for the 10:15 mass.

At 10 o'clock I was on my way to church. I had communion, and I prayed really hard for us, *ma Margot*, and also for our parents. And every moment during the Sanctus, I thought of our engagement …

In the evening, after dinner, I went to the Regent Theatre with the whole gang to see "The Sea Wolf" … and after the movie, we had a few biscuits at a restaurant, with some liquor. No chocolate. And that was hard, because everybody was eating it, and I knew I couldn't have any. This is my sacrifice, and it's a great sacrifice… Always your Jean …

April 17, 1944: Today, there is a change in our activities at Bournemouth. We're having classes, and we'll be starting a three-week course.

This morning, I woke at 6 o'clock because I had an upset stomach, and I had to go to the bathroom and had the trots. Then I couldn't go back to sleep. So I just lay down; I think I had a colic.

After the parade at nine o'clock, we were regrouped again, and I was in the "W 17" … we heard a few speeches and talked about the courses that were to start … From two to three, we did A/C [aircraft] recognition, from three to four we learned about the Marconi radio, and from four to five we did Morse code. Considering that it was the first day of classes, it wasn't too bad. And this is going to continue for the next three weeks ...

April 18, 1944: ... We went to Regent Hall where a Captain, an intelligence officer, briefed us about enemy cannon. It was boring, so I got out of there. However, I almost got caught by a Squadron Leader, but I squeezed by him and got away with it.

In the afternoon ... we went on the roof ... and saw three Typhoons doing low flying. In the last period, we went to recreation ... And then again, like every night, I am faithful to my rendezvous with my *pitoune*, and then I do my rosary. Another day went by. And just like all the others, your Jean is faithful to you, and you can be certain that every night I can say that I have my conscience in hand. Promise. Bye, *ma Margot.*

April 19, 1944: ... classes at the East Cliff Hotel. The first course was aircraft recognition, and for the next two periods it was P.T. During parade, we went to the gym, and ... then we ran for a mile and a half. I was first to get back ... in the evening we played cards, just for fun.

April 20, 1944: ... I was supposed to have breakfast this morning but I only woke up at a quarter after seven. Rather than having breakfast, I prefer to stay in bed till eight ... In the third period, we again went to the Regent. A lot of the guys camouflaged went AWOL, but I followed my intuition. Lucky for me, because a roll call came, and the guys who didn't show up were caught, and they got "C.B." [confined to barracks] for two nights.

At night, I chatted away with my *Margotton*, like I do every evening, and I also wrote to my mother back home … Today like every other day, I had a good one from every point of view, my morale and my health, and like always, I am Jean who is forever the same to his Margot … Bye, *ma Margot.*

April 21, 1944: Today was another great day for me, because this afternoon I received my first letters from Canada. I don't know what I was doing when I received them. All I know is that I took off and ran back to my room, just to read them. I can't remember whether I was crying or laughing. All I was thinking was that I would be happy with what my sweetheart had sent me. I never realized how much my Margot really loved me, and how strongly she loved me, and how much I loved her. And it made me feel so good, every word that I was reading, that my eyes were filling with water. I also got news from home, and I was really happy to know that everything was fine …

This morning, like every morning, I went and did my radio, Morse code and Aldis lamp.

In the afternoon, in the first period, we had another talk by an intelligence officer, and then we were supposed to have aircraft recognition and to finish our Morse code. But instead, we went to listen to some "intermezzo" music and heard some Bing Crosby, Frank Sinatra, etc.

In the evening I went to the Knights of Columbus to iron my suits. I didn't do too badly considering that I never ironed before. No electricity. We had to have a flatiron. What a job!

At noon yesterday, a siren sounded an alert. I had never heard it before … the all-clear came, and nothing really had happened.

April 22, 1944: … we have a new posting. Not really, but it's part of the reserve … Parade at the drill hall, where we had a lecture on parachutes … This afternoon, a special parade for the "postings," and my name was called. I'd rather it wasn't, but I guess it's "His will." But I'm not a reserve, which means that maybe I won't have to stay here. After parade, I took a little ride on my bike … Then I went to church, and felt good there. We talked a little bit, me and my "*Compagnon de route*" …. After supper I decided to go to the movies. We went to the Carlton to see "North Star." I really enjoyed the movie. It was really sad though to see how the Russians were suffering under the Germans. The children were beaten, and the women … it was just too much. I'm happy I'm here to do my duty.

Jean-Maurice in his flying suit. England, 1944.

April 23, 1944: … (Sunday). We went to try on our flying suits, and then we had free time … I got myself to mass. As usual, I took communion and prayed very hard for both of us, for you and me, *ma Margot*. And after mass I played some snooker … After supper, we decided to go to the movies, at the Carlton again. It was "Bad Man" with Henry Aldrich. It wasn't too bad. After that, I went to eat some "French fries and steak" … It is really difficult because I'm missing you so much … *Bye, ma Margotton.*

April 24, 1944: This morning at two o'clock — not very nice, at two o'clock — we were awakened by the air-raid sirens. After we got dressed, we went to our shelter outside. There we could hear the noise of the anti-aircraft guns and the airplane engines. At one point we heard a big sound, and we found ourselves at the bottom of the trenches, with our helmets on our heads. For the first time I realized that I am in a war. The whole thing lasted an hour, and after we went to bed, everything was quiet and peaceful.

At night, because all the guys were together for the last time, we decided that we would have a reunion after the war, on the first of April 1948, at six o'clock, in the lobby of the "Hotel R.A.T. Royal," with the password being "Righty" in the "Limey way."

April 25, 1944: Today there is another change in my military life because we were transferred to a new station, Staverton in Gloucester. This morning, we left Bournemouth at 5:30 to take a train at 9:30. After having travelled for four hours, we arrived at our destination. After we put our bags in a truck and got on another, we were on our way to the camp. We passed by the town and realized that it is big enough and not so bad.

... I really like this camp. It is only five miles from the town and is quite peaceful and quiet. There is also an airport with some really nice airplanes. I saw one called The Devil. It only took us ten minutes, and then we returned to our classes. It's not so bad. In the morning it is pretty cold, though. When it comes to the food, it's pretty good, we eat four times a day: breakfast, lunch, tea and supper. And besides that, we get breaks in the morning and in the after-noon, and we're stuffed.

April 26, 27, 28, 29, 1944: I'm doing a summary because I'm a little behind in my journal. For the first two days, nothing special happened to us. Every day, we go to class until 6 p.m., and in the evening we just sit around in the camp and read or write. On Friday …. we went downtown to the swimming pool for an exercise in the dinghy … then we went for supper at the Café Clarence at Cheltenham. Not bad. We had some sausages and potatoes and green peas. In the evening we went to the movies and saw "Phantom of the Opera." I really enjoyed that …

On Saturday, I went for a bicycle ride around the camp, where the landing strip is, and I was singing away: "*C'elle que j'aime*" and "*Elle que j'adore*" ….

April 30, 1944: … Like every Sunday night, I am ending up talking to you, my *Margotton*, and with the temperature being ideal, I would love to talk about the past with my little fiancée. I can't wait to see you … in the little town I noticed how much of it reminded me of you. From your *'tit Jean* … I looked at the others, and it was very typical that I was thinking of you, my little treasure. I am yours, my little one. Bye, *ma pitoune.*

May 2, 1944: … we practised parachute jumping, how to fall, etc. That was fun, and it is also very important … At night we played a little bit of cards. Now I'm starting to like it a bit more because we're playing for money. But my budget doesn't allow me to lose too many times …

… during the last two periods, we worked on navigation, and I found that very interesting. I sort of like that. In the afternoon, our first two courses were on the "rubicals." I had a hard time with this, but it was quite interesting to be the receiver … We went down to Cheltenham for a swim. I am still in good shape. By 5:30, I returned to the camp. I didn't stay in town, because then we'd end up hanging around for the movies at night, and that means about ten shillings, and my budget doesn't allow me to do this. The main reason is that I'd rather go back to the camp and write to you, *ma pitoune* ...

May 3, 4 & 5, 1944: I have to summarize because I am a little bit behind ... we had some courses on how to do parachute jumping, with practising flips and balancing, how to fall, etc. That was fun. And also, I know it's going to be necessary at one point.

May 6, 1944: Saturday. Today is our day off ... Went to Gloucester and took my washing ... took the bus and returned to Cheltenham. There I tried to have my picture taken, but everything was closed ....

May 7, 1944: ... in the morning I went to church at Insworth; I prayed for you, *ma Margotton*. In the afternoon, for the first time, we flew over England. It lasted about 2 hours and 45 minutes ...

May 9, 1944: After leaving Staverton at about 8 in the morning, we went to Morton Valence. We're going to be there. It's ... about an hour away, about 16 miles. When we got there, I wasn't really impressed because it's so far away. The mess hall, the airport, the barracks, etc. In all, it was quite a good walk. But I think I'm going to like it because it's in the open country, it's quiet, peaceful, and since I can spend more time with *Margotton*, I like this place.

May 10, 1944: Today in class; and in the morning we flew, and — as usual — long trips. Three hours in the afternoon, then in class, then we came back to rest in the barracks.

May 12, 1944: ... I took pictures, so I can send them to you, *ma pitoune*. In the afternoon, I went down to Cheltenham by jeep. There, I bought some postcards. I also tried to get my watch fixed, but there was no way. I went to see the movie "Captain Blood," and then in the evening, I ate at the YMCA. To go back, the Americans gave me a lift in the jeep.

May 13, 1944: … I have a little bit of the blues …

May 14, 1944: Sunday. For the first time, I didn't go to mass today. I missed it because we were flying in the morning, and in the afternoon, we had class. Instead, we spread out in the sun …

May 15, 1944: This morning, for the second time, I woke up with the sirens announcing an air raid. It was about two a.m. We weren't affected because it was all the way out in Bristol. Nevertheless, we heard the sirens, and we could see the search lights, and we could hear some of the explosions, but it didn't last very long. When we went to bed, we heard the JU 88s passing over us …

May 16, 1944: … we were supposed to go flying, but it was a "wash out."

May 18, 1944: … I am fairly happy because I got to see the padre. We talked for a while, and I went to confession in the afternoon. I went to mass, and I went to communion, and I prayed real hard for you, *ma Margotton*. Also, I saw the Educational Officer, whose job it is to take care of our troubles. Since I want to enrol in the technical drawing course, I spoke to him and had a discussion about the mechanical drawing engineer program … I was thinking that later on, in our future, I could make you so happy, because with that I could work really hard, and I am going to succeed. You'll see how happy we're going to be in our home. We're going to be happy. I will love you forever …

May 19, 1944: ... our sergeant's stripes are well earned. In one word: we are good in class, and we're not working too much.

What was really my great surprise: I received a letter from you, *ma Margotton*. It had been a month since I last received one. And boy, did it ever feel good. My heart was beating really fast. In the evening, right up to two o'clock in the morning, I read your letter. A good day ...

May 20, 1944: Since we are flying a bit later in the evening, we got to sleep in, and we got the day off. I didn't get up till lunch time ... In the afternoon, we were supposed to be flying, but since the weather was very bad, the flying was cancelled, and we went back to barracks ... I played cards, and I won. I made about a dollar. I was really lucky. Another good day ...

May 21, 1944: A truck took me downtown for the 9:15 mass. It was a beautiful little church in the old style, but really religious. I really prayed hard for you, *ma Margotton*. I had communion ... during the Sanctus I thought also of the time when we were

engaged before God, and every time I think of that, I get closer, I'm quite moved. After mass, I also lit a candle for you because we only get what we want after we light a candle ... I went to see a movie downtown at the Hippodrome and saw "Chad Hanna" in technicolor, with Dorothy Lamour and Henry Fonda.

There was a "show" performed by the RCAF, and it was really good. I think for the first time since I left you, *ma Margotton*, I laughed so hard, it

Jean-Maurice D'Avril in Cheltenham, England, 1944.

felt so good. But I was thinking of the olden days with you, whenever we'd be together, we would tickle each other, and we laughed so much that I cried, just to defend myself. Those were such good times.

May 22, 1944: Another day of flying … At the briefing room, we received our instructions, our decoding … It was a beautiful day, and it was a very good trip. Again today, I got some mail, but this time it was two letters from home, one dated

Jean-Maurice and fiancée Margot, Montreal, early 1944.

the 2nd and the other the 8th of May. I was really happy to find out that no one was sick and everything was going well … But only the letters from my *Margotton* are the best for my heart. My *Margotton* is in my heart …

May 23, 1944: … we got ready and had our supper because tonight we're flying.

Tonight we're flying, and we're going to do the first complete tour. But on our second trip, since the temperature was really bad, we came back down at 3 o'clock. So after four and a half hours of flying, when I fell into my bed at 4:30, it felt really good …

I'm saving myself for you, for our future because I never want to have regrets about anything …

May 24, 1944: Wednesday. Another great day because … I received four beautiful letters from my *Margotton* this afternoon, dated the 17th, 24th, 26th and 28th … I read them

more than once, from one end to the other. I was smiling …
sometimes I was serious, sometimes I had tears in the corner of my eyes …

May 25, 1944: Thursday. Today, I received mail again, a letter from the 6th of May. Does it ever feel good to see those letters from you, *ma Margotton*, after waiting so long … This morning I got paid. I received three pounds twelve because now we're starting to pay for our Victory Bonds, but it seems to be enough.

After lunch I decided to go down to Cheltenham to get my pictures. I went down in a jeep, and I came back in a jeep, always hitchhiking. I like that, it's fun. Then I was very happy with my pictures because they turned out really well. I'm anxious to send them to you as soon as possible …

In the evening, I was supposed to go flying, but because of the temperature, it was washed out. I wasn't upset; I didn't feel like doing it.

Another day has gone by, and again everything went well. Just enough time to do my rosary. I will always be the same to you, *ma Margotton*. Only for you alone, I promise. I love you. Bye, *ma pitoune*.

This was Jean-Maurice D'Avril's last diary entry.

CHAPTER 17

Sixty Years Later

Mar arch 2005. I am aboard an aircraft flying through the dark night from west to east. This aircraft is not a bomber, but an Air Canada Airbus A 330. I study the data sheet in the pouch in front of me. The ten-year-old A 330 has a seating capacity of 252 passengers including the cockpit crew of two and the cabin crew of eleven men and women. If it were a cargo plane, its capacity would be 16,769 kilograms. We are flying at a cruising speed of 870 km/h and an altitude of 11,000 metres. The plane has a range of 12,400 kilometres. The plane is on its way from Toronto to Frankfurt, a distance of 6,750 kilometres, which it will cover in about eight-and-a-half hours.

There are many technical differences between this flight and the last flight of the *Q Queen*. That plane had been commissioned only a month earlier. It carried a crew of seven and a bomb load of eight tons (about 8,000 kilograms), about half the cargo capacity of this airliner. The *Q Queen's* air speed when fully loaded was 280 km/h, although when diving, it could reach a speed of over 500 km/h. On its way to the target city, it would fly at an altitude of 18,000 feet (about 5,500 metres). It took just under four hours to reach Chemnitz, a flying distance of about 1,100 kilometres from the base in Tholthorpe, Yorkshire.

I place myself in Jean-Maurice's position and contemplate the other differences between our flights. His world was the bloodiest war in history. We are at peace. At least, there is no major armed conflict anywhere that is even remotely comparable to World War II. I am confident that this plane will touch down more or less on schedule, and that I will catch a connecting flight to Dresden in comfort and safety. There will be no night fighters and no flak waiting for us over Germany. The probability of surviving this flight is virtually 100 percent.

When Jean-Maurice sat in his cramped seat as a wireless operator/air gunner in the Halifax, his chance of survival was considerably less. The seven young men in the rattling, roaring aircraft, flying toward the target together with over 700 other heavy bombers, had to expect death, although they were conditioned not to let the thought of death interfere with their determination and their technical skills as airmen. As they were approaching the target

Jean-Maurice D'Avril beside a Halifax bomber.

Chemnitz after the bombing.

city, brightly illuminated and marked by the Pathfinders, they concentrated on doing the job for which they had been trained. They did their duty. My flight is between two continents at peace. Jean-Maurice's flight was between two countries at war. My flight is between two worlds that are almost interchangeable: both provide comfortable, safe living conditions for the vast majority of citizens. In 1945, the world of England — a democracy that had survived in spite of incredible odds — and the world of Germany — a dictatorship at the brink of destruction — were aeons apart.

Chemnitz, March 5, 2005

We are standing in the "New Market Square" in Chemnitz, my cousin Fritz, Lise and Jean Desjardins, and I. Behind us is the new city hall (built in the 1890s). Around the corner is the old city hall, a structure dating back to the Renaissance. Both buildings were severely damaged sixty years ago today and later restored.

Sixty years ago on this day and throughout the night, the inner city of Chemnitz was destroyed by Bomber Command and the 8th U.S. Army Air Force in Operation Thunderclap. There is snow on the ground, just as there was 60 years ago. Perhaps a 100 people have gathered in this square, waiting for the anniversary commemoration to start. Most are seniors. A handful of teenagers stand around in a cluster, talking to each other, joking, laughing, as teenagers do the world over.

I try to understand what a small group of Chemnitz artists are doing. Two performers are wearing costumes. One, a figure on stilts, about three metres tall, obviously acts as Death. The other, a fat, ugly figure, staggers around and less obviously represents a soldier, war, and violence. He is dressed in modern camouflage fatigues and wears a funny brown cap. He could be taken for an American in Iraq or Afghanistan, but only with some imagination. He certainly doesn't look like any soldier from World War II. While Death stalks around in silence, Soldier, also silent, struts back and forth rather aimlessly — a clown. Funeral music plays over a loudspeaker. Then the music stops, and there is a moment of silence.

An announcement is made from the middle of the square, but the acoustics are flawed, and the words are muffled. No one around us can make it out. Now, a big white kite is carried into the square. It looks like a tent with waving, sail-like wings, and represents an airplane. The people carrying the kite drop it on the ground and set fire to it. At the same time, Soldier either falls or is pushed to the ground, near the smoking remnants of the kite. He remains silent and crumpled on the ground.

A single bell tolls from the nearby tower of St-Jacob's Church just behind the old city hall. I remember that the church and its tower were smouldering ruins after the attack. High up on the balustrade, a *türmer* (a watchman on a tower) appears and calls out a warning cry. There were no tower watchmen in 1945, only air-raid wardens with megaphones and field telephones. The sound of an air-raid siren comes over the loudspeaker. It is the long, even sound of the all-clear, not the rapidly undulating, nerve-racking alert that wailed from dozens of rooftops to announce an imminent air raid.

I am sure that the artists who organized this "happening" in the market square meant well. However, they fail to convey whatever message they set out to communicate. Lise and Jean, too, are merely puzzled. What is going on? The few people who have come are wondering instead of commemorating.

A large tent in the form of a cross has been erected in the square. Inside is a table with pencils and paper. People are encouraged to write down their thoughts and pin them to the walls of the tent. Many of the notes contain anti-war messages relevant to 2005 rather than 1945. I see several that refer to Iraq. Among the most relevant thoughts I see pinned to the tent walls is this anonymous message:

Wir müssen das Gestern beweinen,
auf das Morgen setzen
und den Hass von heute bekämpfen.

Let us cry for yesterday,
hope for tomorrow
and fight hatred today.

Although we suffer from jetlag, we go back to the square that night. The newspapers had announced that all the bells in the city would toll at the precise moment when the attack started 60 years ago. The attendees were asked to come and bring candles to light. There was to be "a sea of light," to symbolize the firestorm that raged in the city, but also to signal hope for a peaceful future.

I am disappointed, and embarrassed for Lise and Jean to see that the people of Chemnitz stay home by the thousands. Fritz's wife, Irmgard, has come along this time, and she has brought five candles. There are another fifty or so, and there is no sea of light, only a puddle of light on the pavement stones, with a small cluster of people standing around in thought. It is a touching vigil, but the numbers speak volumes. Commemorating the 60th anniversary of the knockout blow against their city is not high on the list of priorities for Chemnitzers tonight.

To be fair, there are some indoor activities elsewhere. I read the next day that those were well-attended. I had expected thousands in the streets, dozens of sirens wailing, and all the bells of the city's many churches ringing simultaneously. My expectations were not met. The sea of light did not materialize.

Life goes on in Chemnitz where unemployment is at an outrageous 18.8 percent. Virtually all factories were shut down shortly after reunification, and only their empty shells — and a museum of industry — are reminders of the city's former role as one of Germany's major industrial centres. The city's population has dropped by almost 20 percent since reunification. When I lived in Chemnitz as a child, the population was 350,000. By the end of World War II, it was down to 250,000. As Karl-Marx-Stadt (1953 to 1990), the city grew again to over 300,000 inhabitants. Today's population of Chemnitz is only 246,000, and that in spite of the fact that eight outlying communities have been annexed by the city since 1994.[1] Clearly, the people of Chemnitz are more concerned about the present and the future than about the past.

Frankenberg, March 6, 2005

One of the main reasons Lise and Jean Desjardins and I have come to Germany is to help unveil the plaque commemorating the murder of Jean-Maurice D'Avril. The event is scheduled for 10 a.m.

The plaque itself has its history. When I was in Germany in October 2004, I was invited to attend a meeting of the Frankenberg *Heimatverein* (historical society). I talked about the murder of the "nameless Canadian airman" and my quest for his identity. The original idea, to rename Äussere Freiberger Strasse, where the murder occurred, in honour of Jean-Maurice D'Avril, was soon abandoned. It was thought that the town council would never concur, since "there had been far too many changes of street names in recent history." It is true that a large number of streets in the former East Germany had been named to commemorate prominent Nazis and persons held in high esteem by the Nazis. After the war these streets were given the names of prominent Communists. After reunification the names were changed again. But the historical society thought that a commemorative cairn and plaque at the murder site would be a good idea as a gesture of remorse and reconciliation. The local newspaper reported on the meeting and the plans for a monument.

Over the months that followed, I corresponded with the society's president, Dietmar Palm. They planned for quite an ambitious monument, with a Saxon sandstone base 150 centimetres high and a bronze plaque, to be erected on town property, right at the murder site at the corner of Äussere Freiberger Strasse and Amalienstrasse. However, a request to Frankenberg's town council for a financial contribution to the monument was voted down unanimously. The reason for the denial: "We already have several stones and monuments commemorating the victims of both world wars in Frankenberg. The Town Council is of the opinion that tribute to all victims is therefore paid in a dignified fashion." This also meant that the site on town property was no longer available. It now turned out that the society itself had no money to pay for a cairn, a stone, or even a plaque. I was asked to look for funding in Canada.

At first, I was reluctant to do this. After all, the plaque was to be an initiative coming from the citizens of Frankenberg. I was tempted to suggest that the society scrap the project, but they told me they had already obtained an agreement from a local firm willing to donate the engraving. Worse, I had told Lise Desjardins about their plans, and we had made arrangements to attend the unveiling. I approached a number of Canadian organizations including the Air Force Association in Ottawa, the RCAF POW Association, the Bomber Command Association of Canada, and the 425 (Alouette) Squadron Association. They all turned me down.

The project was saved by Dominion Command of the Royal Canadian Legion in Ottawa. After the local legion branch in Arnprior

sponsored the application, Dominion Command paid $400 toward
the plaque. Material for the stand and all the work was supplied by
volunteers in Frankenberg, and the engraving was done gratis by the
firm of Walzengravur in Frankenberg. Another donation for the
project came from John Gendron of Bill Mitchell's crew.

The historical society mailed invitations for the unveiling cere-
mony to its members, all the eyewitnesses in and near Frankenberg,
and in Drebach, all members of Frankenberg's town council, and
others who had shown an interest in the story. The general public
was invited through a newspaper article.

Addi Jacobi, a Chemnitz journalist, communicated the story of
the murder, my investigation, the forthcoming unveiling of the
commemorative plaque, and the visit by the victim's family
members to the TV network *MDR (Mitteldeutscher Rundfunk)* in
Dresden. Their reporter, Nils Werner, called me before I left for
Germany, and they decided to televise the unveiling. Nils Werner
phoned me again in Chemnitz. "Please be at the site an hour
before the unveiling."

Fritz and Irmgard Neidhardt, Lise and Jean Desjardins, and I
arrive at the murder site in Frankenberg at 9 a.m. It is a cold, blus-
tery Sunday morning. The temperature hovers around -15
Celsius. There is a strong wind, and blowing snow soon covers us
all in a thick, white blanket. We first walk to the wooden fence at
the corner. As Lise touches the fence, I know that something
touches her. I show Lise and Jean where Jean-Maurice walked
with the guard, coming from the army barracks, and exactly
where he was ambushed. I point out where he crawled across the
street, and where he died in a pool of blood. It is as if we are re-
enacting the gruesome and tragic events, 60 years later, almost to
the hour. No one says a word.

The TV crew (Nils Werner, a cameraman, and a young woman
responsible for the production), arrives in a van. I introduce Lise
and Jean. We are asked to walk up and down the street a few times
for the camera. Werner interviews us. Soon others arrive: Diet-

mar Palm and his wife; Wolfgang Hammer, whose grandfather was the policeman in charge of the civilian "investigation" that led nowhere; Marion Rau, the Frankenberg archivist. Two eyewitnesses to the murder, Ulrich Köhler and Elfriede Rupprecht, arrive. There is silent reflection on all sides as Lise meets a man and a woman who saw her brother die.

The other eyewitnesses declined the invitation for health reasons. Another cameraman arrives: cable TV from Chemnitz. Andreas Luksch of the *Freie Presse* is there. I am pleased to see a large crowd. I observe that there are almost as many people assembled here, in little Frankenberg, as there were yesterday in the market square in Chemnitz.

Dietmar Palm opens the proceedings. He says that the plaque will serve as a reminder that the barbarism of World War II had reached even this small town, that by identifying and naming this young victim, that sad period of the town's history is losing some of its anonymity. He unveils the shiny trilingual brass plaque, which reads:

Hier wurde im März 1945 der kanadische Kriegsgefangene
RCAF-Leutnant Jean-Maurice D'Avril (22)
hinterhältig erschlagen.
Wir trauern um ihn und alle Kriegsopfer

Here, the Canadian prisoner of war,
RCAF P/O Jean-Maurice D'Avril (22),
was cowardly beaten to death in March 1945.
We mourn him and all victims of war

C'est ici que le prisonnier de guerre canadien,
Jean-Maurice D'Avril (22 ans), slt, A.R.C.,
fut odieusement battu à mort en mars 1945.
Nous pleurons sa perte et celle de toutes les victimes de guerre

Just in time for the unveiling, a large delegation arrives from Drebach. They explain that a snowstorm dumped fifteen centimetres of snow in the night. There had been thick fog early in the morning, but Hermann Pährisch says: "It would take more than a little bit of snow and fog to stop real Ore Mountains people from coming to an event like this!"

All the Drebach eyewitnesses are there: Pährisch, Egon Lötzsch, Achim Hartmann, Manfred Heeg, Lothar Ficker, and Eberhard Gerlach. Some have brought their wives. I introduce them all to Lise and Jean. They have come to honour the Canadian who tragically lost his life after bailing out of the plane that crashed near their home village. Lise thanks them for their kindness.

Egon Lötzsch says: "If your brother had come down near us in the Ore Mountains, he might still be alive today." Lise shakes his hand.

In addition to the invited guests, some people have come because they read the article about the event in the local paper. Conspicuous by their absence are members of the Frankenberg town council. Andreas Luksch of the *Freie Presse* asks Dietmar Palm: "How do you feel about the fact that the Town didn't help and also didn't send anyone?" Palm answers by remaining silent. Luksch later describes it in his article as an "icy silence." We talk about the irony that the alleged leader of the assailants had been a member of Frankenberg town council during the Third Reich. Someone remarks: "You can bet that if elections were going to be held next week, they'd all be here." There are many similarities between Germany and Canada.

I say a few words, thank those who have come in spite of the bad weather, and introduce Lise and Jean. Lise's voice trembles. She apologizes that she can't speak German. I apologize that as a Canadian I can't understand enough French to interpret from Lise's mother tongue. She speaks in English.

"Usually when a soldier dies, he is buried, and that's when his story comes to an end. Although I was very young when Jean-Maurice died, painful memories of my brother have always

remained in my heart. Too many questions were unanswered ...
I would have never thought it possible that I would some day
have the experience of being in Germany, here at this public
place. I find it difficult to express my emotions, and yet a simple
thanks seems inadequate for this great gift you have given me in
memory of my brother. I am eternally grateful for the honour
you have bestowed on him today."

Lise is a brave woman and manages to hold back her tears till
the very end. Jean comforts her. As the TV cameras roll, a car
drives by at high speed, windows open. Some young men inside
shout, "Bomb attack!" They are gone in a flash. Brave enough to
make a statement, too cowardly to be identified.

All of us, including the TV crews, move out of the snow into
the warmth of a nearby restaurant for a reception. Here, the TV
crews take close-ups of photos I have brought with me. They
interview Lise, Jean, and me again. The *MDR* crew also drives up
to Drebach in spite of the bad weather and takes shots at the
crash site. Their material is condensed into a 10-minute documentary to be shown all across Germany the following week.

After the reception, Marion Rau invites our small party of five
to the archives where she serves us cappuccino in the research
room. She had initially planned to hold the reception there for
everyone attending the unveiling, but had to switch to the restaurant after the mayor had objected: "That's not what the archives
is for." The archives is not an independent institution, but a section of the municipal administration. She shows Lise and Jean
some of the documents which helped me last year to discover
Jean-Maurice's identity. Lise places her hands on the book of
cemetery records the way one touches a family bible.

After a tour of the seventeenth-century archives building, Frau
Rau presents Lise and Jean with some large reproductions of
Frankenberg prints. She gives me a print of a watercolour showing
the Frankenberg market square on the day in May 1945 when it was
occupied by American troops. Had it not been for my curiosity

"I do not like being in the public eye." The author and Lise Desjardins visit eyewitness Anni Bodenschatz (middle) on March 6, 2005.

about American troops in Frankenberg, I would have never stumbled across the murder of the "unknown Canadian airman." Lise Desjardins believes in destiny. Perhaps she is right. I invite the archivist to join us for lunch at a very *gemütlich* restaurant.

Before leaving Frankenberg, we pay a visit to Frau Bodenschatz, another eyewitness to the murder. She did not attend the unveiling although she lives just around the corner from the site. She says: "I do not like being in the public eye." I fully understand. There are still secrets in this small town. However, she does not mind posing for a photograph with "the Canadians." Frau Bodenschatz recalls some of her memories for the benefit of Lise and Jean. She tells them how sorry she is now and how shocked she was at the time, 60 years ago.

Berlin, March 9, 2005

This is the first time I meet Dr Ulrich Koch. Of course, I had many long telephone conversations with him, including the half-hour discussion that led to this book, back in February 2004, when he said: "By the way, did you know that ...?"

Koch comes to meet us at the hotel. He is comfortable to be

addressed as Dr Koch, and we oblige. Dr Koch is not at all how I imagined him from our phone and e-mail contacts. He is not yet 60, rather short than tall, of slight build. With his neatly trimmed grey beard, his short-cropped hair, and his keen eyes that are constantly on the move, he reminds me of a private detective or a hotel manager. If I were to cast an actor to play the role of Koch, I would pick the late Peter Sellers or perhaps Dustin Hoffman. He talks very quickly, but he obviously thinks even faster. He jumps easily from subject to subject, occasionally losing focus. Good thing he does, since that is how I learned about the "unknown Canadian airman" murdered in Frankenberg. I sometimes have the feeling that he is leaving me behind, especially since I am trying to interpret for Lise and Jean as we go along. I just can't talk that fast. I am surprised and somewhat disappointed that he doesn't speak English. He shows us some of the major sites around Museum Island and Unter den Linden. It is as cold in Berlin as it was in Saxony, and I am glad to have my Canadian parka. When a sudden squall dumps wet snow on us, we first seek refuge in the *Berliner Dom* (Berlin Cathedral) and finally retreat to the Opera Café for coffee and cake.

Lise and I have brought lettered red and white ribbons from Canada for the three wreaths we are going to lay at Jean-Maurice D'Avril's grave: one from Lise and her family (*"avec amour"*); one from me (*"nameless no more"*); and one from John Gendron. Dr Koch has ordered them for us, and we are to bring the ribbons to be attached today. I ask him when the flower shop closes. He says there is plenty of time, and insists on showing us yet another site and yet another monument and yet another architectural gem. It is after dark when he finally decides it's time to head for the flower shop, which is near his home. I hadn't realized how far it would be. We walk to the S-Bahn (light-rail) station and buy return tickets. We have to change trains somewhere. I become confused because there are so many lines and stops and names to remember. Koch insists that it will be easy to find the way back. "You can't miss it." But I make another plan.

It is a very long walk from the S-Bahn station in some completely out-of-the-way part of Berlin to the flower shop. We arrive two minutes before closing time. The girl kindly agrees to work overtime to attach the ribbons, which takes some time. The wreaths are made of soft cedar boughs, decorated with red and white roses. We pay for them and say "Good night" to Dr Koch, "see you in the morning." I ask the girl to call us a cab. I gladly pay the driver 12 euro, and we throw the return rail tickets away.

Berlin, March 10, 2005

I take the BMW rental car I parked in the hotel courtyard and squeeze it through the narrow passage way out into Linienstrasse. I am glad to have Koch in the front seat to guide me through Berlin traffic from Oranienburger Tor in the former East Berlin to Charlottenburg in the former West Berlin. I park the car on Heerstrasse, right in front of the cemetery, whose official name is "Berlin 1939–1945 War Cemetery."

At 10:30 sharp, a van pulls up in front of my car. The driver opens the doors for representatives of the Canadian Embassy who are attending the wreath laying. They are Minister-Counsellor Chris Greenshields (political and public affairs), Navy Captain Stuart Andrews (military attaché), and Thilo Lenz (public affairs attaché). They are bringing Father (Major) Z. Gracjan Burkiciak (Roman Catholic chaplain for the Canadian Armed Forces in Europe).

Lise, Jean, and I place our wreaths at the base of Jean-Maurice D'Avril's gravestone. They are the only things of bright colour in the stark black and white scenery of this cemetery. We all stand in the snow on this cold morning in Berlin with our heads bowed. Again, I see in my mind's eye the studio photo of the handsome young Canadian airman that had

Of the 3,580 war graves, 527 belong to Canadians, mostly airmen.

caused him an ominous premonition.

With his charming Polish accent, Father Burkiciak reads words that would have pleased Jean-Maurice D'Avril and that I know bring comfort to Lise and Jean:

Three wreaths at Jean-Maurice's grave: one from the Desjardins family, one from the author, and one from RCAF veteran John Gendron.

> Loving Father, listen to our prayers as we remember Jean-Maurice ... We thank you for the good things you have done for us and in his life. Grant that he may be with you in heaven ...
>
> Bless his grave and our brother Jean-Maurice, and send Your Holy Angel to watch over him ...

Others pray in silence. Lise has fallen to her knees, her black cape in sharp contrast to the white snow.

CHAPTER 18

A sk Them for Forgiveness ...

Reconciliation may not feel just, but it is right just the same.

Bruce Edwards in "Africa after the Wars,"
CBC program on *The Current*, December 29, 2004

I am at the end of my journey of discovery and pleased that I was able to find some truths. I was deeply involved in this case. Throughout this exercise, I felt an inner force that compelled me to go on and to set aside other priorities. It has been a very emotional experience for me. I have had my moments of doubt, and I sometimes wondered whether the results would justify my enormous effort, my three trips to Germany, my extensive travel in Canada, the thousands of hours I put into this venture. The story of Jean-Maurice D'Avril has become part of my life.

As I researched and wrote the account of this murder, my personal memories played an important role, emerging as I unravelled the realities of the bombing and the murder. Now, I feel satisfied that I have met a challenge. I have climbed the main peak of this mountain. Although I regret that there are routes I was unable to take, routes that might have led to even more discoveries, I am happy to have brought a little more light into the darkness surrounding a tragic event.

What about the killers of Jean-Maurice D'Avril, the murderers who were never brought to justice? I was never able to discover more than strong hints and rumours about them. The involvement of the two men whose names came up could not be proven. They are both long dead. Others may never be named unless a police investigation is launched, which seems highly unlikely.

But I have learned much, not only about the murder case and the events of the war, but also about myself. My own attitude and perspective have undergone a change. I look differently at Canada and its role in World War II.

In the first few years after I arrived in Canada, I sometimes shrugged contemptuously when early November and "poppy time" came around. I belittled or even ridiculed Canadians who wore such visible reminders on their lapels in the weeks leading up to Remembrance Day and then gathered at war memorials across the country to remember their countrymen who had died in the two world wars. "Only 42,000 Canadian soldiers were killed in World War II? Why, that's nothing in comparison with European dimensions."

However, in the process of researching and writing this book, I have come to realize how meaningless such comparisons are. The experience of Canadian soldiers who were wounded and who suffered as prisoners of war was just as real as the experience of Europeans in the same position. No one should play a numbers game when it comes to human agony.

Wartime mentality caused by high-pitch propaganda and the escalation of revenge following the ever-mounting number of family members killed — soldiers in the field and bombing victims at home — led to a dehumanizing equalization of "willingness" on both sides. The concept of eye for eye, tooth for tooth, became a driving force in Nazi Germany as well as in Allied countries. Germans became willing to sanction, condone, and even participate in illegal and immoral acts, from air attacks on London to the execution of Jews in gas chambers. Britons and their "imperial" Allies became willing to approve and encourage what they perceived as justice: the creation of firestorms in German cities. Japanese became willing to torture prisoners of war, and Americans became willing to accept the use of atomic bombs on two Japanese cities. In Frankenberg, a small handful of minor Nazi functionaries became willing to club a young Canadian airman to death. All

The Strategic Bomber Offensive — despicable but understandable.

these acts were related. All were despicable. All were understandable in the context of the times. The results were the same: the violent death of human beings. The sentiments expressed in the quotation below are perhaps shared by many of those Canadians who know about Canada's participation in Bomber Command at all:

The Strategic Bomber Offensive was one of the most controversial campaigns in the Second World War. Today it is hard to imagine the reasons for bombing cities when it is known thousands of civilians, women and children, would die, but to judge the circumstances of 1944 you have to understand the times in which the decision was made ... The atrocities committed on the people of Europe by Adolf

Hitler, the mass murders, the extermination of millions, were beyond the comprehension of a normal person ... From 1939 to 1943, Hitler had been very close to winning the war ... Desperate situations call for desperate measures, and it is from defeat that Bomber Command was born. Brutality is a part of war, and when fighting against the most brutal of enemies, there can be no quarter ... There is no high moral road in war.[1]

As I have tried to document in this book, the Allies — including Canadians — killed many thousands of innocent men, women, and children through the deliberate, merciless bombing of residential areas of cities. The Soviet Union's police and military forces left a trail of blood and horror in the German territories they occupied early in 1945 as well as in the eastern parts of Poland they occupied in 1939. Poles, Czechs, and Yugoslavs took bloody revenge on German civilians at the end of the war and after the war. In summary, the Allies and former enemies of Germany are also guilty of war crimes. But can and should these atrocities be compared with the insanity and obscenity of hate-inspired racism? Can they excuse the bloody orgy of genocidal mass extermination that swept across Europe, ordered and directed by a criminal German regime and carried out by its obedient servants?

We should shudder to think what kind of a world would have emerged had Nazi Germany won World War II. Six million Jews were slaughtered between 1941 and 1945. A German victory under Hitler would have spelled a disaster of even greater proportions. Millions more would have been dispossessed, enslaved, sterilized, and eventually exterminated. Hitler and his military machine had to be stopped by force. That — in my opinion — made World War II a "necessary war" for the Allies, or to quote Jack Granatstein, "The Last Good War."

Yet this realization should not make anyone proud of the retaliatory methods used by the Allies. Individual soldiers, airmen, and sailors — in Canada and other Allied countries — had every reason and every right to be proud of their bravery and sacrifice. They fought valiantly for their countries, their beliefs and values. Yet they, too, were used as pawns in a deadly chess game directed on both sides by ruthless political and military leaders who wanted to win at any price. And the price was high, not only in lives, but also in honour. There can be no honour in burning children alive. As there can be no honour in bludgeoning a young prisoner of war.

This cross, eight metres high, now crowns the cupola of Dresden's Frauenkirche. *It was made in England as a "symbol of suffering and reconciliation."*

The Duke of Kent, in addressing the citizens of Dresden on February 13, 2000, called a large cross made in Britain for the reconstructed *Frauenkirche* in Dresden "a symbol of suffering and reconciliation." The time has come to recognize and acknowledge that Canadians caused great suffering in Germany, and that Germans caused great suffering to Canadians. Such an acknowledgement is a first step toward reconciliation. Jean-Maurice D'Avril and the nearly 10,000 other Canadians who perished in Bomber Command did not die in vain. Their loss taught us a lesson. Their memory can serve us as well.

There can be no reconciliation, no forgiveness, without acknowledgement and atonement. In Germany, Lise and Jean Desjardins and I experienced this on a personal level. Elfriede Rupprecht, one of the German eyewitnesses to the murder in Frankenberg, expressed it well in a letter she wrote to me after I interviewed her:

All Germans became guilty through the brutality and cruelty of the Nazi regime. And yet, there were many people here who condemned these cruelties. The bombs which the airmen dropped on our cities also did not discriminate between soldiers, women and children, or seniors. This fact motivated some unscrupulous individuals to take advantage of the resulting hatred and rage. In their perversity they took the law into their own hands. Yet undoubtedly the airman they killed had believed he was only doing his duty.

If you have an opportunity, please tell any surviving family members of the murder victim how truly sorry I am. Ask them for forgiveness in the name of many Germans who share my sentiments.[2]

"All those families deprived ..." The D'Avril family of Montreal in 1944.

Her sentiments were shared by the many witnesses who came forward and others in Germany who helped me find the truth about what happened to Jean-Maurice, and ultimately, to bring that truth home to his family. But I'll give the last word to Lise. In a letter she sent me just before Christmas 2004, in anticipation of our trip to Germany together, she wrote:

I'm about to make a very important discovery: to learn the truth about the last episodes in my brother's life ... I can't wait to read your book, which will make the history of our family more complete. My parents always detested war. All those sons and fathers killed, all those families deprived of their humanity. I do not like war.

I want to thank those German people who were eye-witnesses to these events and who have come forward to make it possible for this true story to be written. I also want to thank my brother's last comrade in arms for his contribution. And finally, thanks to you for having given me an opportunity to know the truth.

– Lise D'Avril, December 2004

APPENDIX I

Abbreviations

CBC	Canadian Broadcasting Corporation
C.V.S.M.	Canadian Volunteer Service Medal
CWCIU	Canadian War Crimes Investigation Unit
CWGC	Commonwealth War Graves Commission
DFC	Distinctive Flying Cross
DND	Department of National Defence (Canada)
FFAF	Free French Air Force
F/Lt	flight lieutenant
F/O	flying officer
F/S or F/Sgt.	flight sergeant
GDR	German Democratic Republic (former East Germany)
Gestapo	Secret State Police (*Geheime Staatspolizei*)
H2S	radar system (Bomber Command)
M/U/G	mid-upper gunner
NSDAP	National Socialist Workers Party (Nazi Party)
PFF	Pathfinder Force

P/O	pilot officer
Q Queen	Halifax III *PN-173*, coded *KW-Q*
POW	prisoner of war
RAAF	Royal Australian Air Force
RAF	Royal Air Force
RCAF	Royal Canadian Air Force
RNZAF	Royal New Zealand Air Force
R/G	rear gunner
SA	Storm Troopers (*Sturmabteilung*)
SD	Security Service of the SS (*Sicherheitsdienst*)
Sgt	sergeant
SS	Nazi Elite Guard (*Schutzstaffel*)
Stalag	main POW camp (*Stammlager*)
USAAF	U.S. Army Air Force
V-1, V-2	guided rocket bombs (V for *Vergeltung* [Revenge])
WAG	wireless operator/ air gunner
W/O	wireless operator
WWII	World War II (1939–1945)

APPENDIX II

Timeline of Key World War II Events Relevant to Bombing Operations

an example of deadly escalation in war

1939

August 28	Germany and Soviet Union sign non-aggression treaty.
September 1	Germany attacks Poland from the west.
September 3	Great Britain and France declare war on Germany.
September 10	Canada declares war on Germany.
September 17	Soviet Union attacks Poland from the east.
September 19	Heavy German bombing raids on Warsaw.
October 6	Poland surrenders. Hitler offers peace to Great Britain and France.
Sep. '39 to May '40	"*Sitzkrieg*" [Phoney War] on the western front.

1940

April 9	German troops occupy Denmark and Norway.

May 10	Germany attacks France, occupies the Netherlands and Belgium.
	Winston Churchill becomes British Prime Minister.
	British aircraft attack military targets in Germany, also causing some civilian deaths.
	The Luftwaffe mistakenly drops bombs on the German city of Freiburg, causing 57 civilian deaths. Hitler blames the attack on Great Britain (first use of the term "terror attack").
June	Several British bombing raids against Hamburg.
June 10	Italy enters the war on Germany's side.
June 22	France surrenders.
July 10	Beginning of Luftwaffe air attacks on Britain.
July 19	Hitler proposes peace with Great Britain, which rejects the offer.
August 1	Hitler orders "intensified air war."
August 13	"Eagle Day": 2,355 German aircraft attack targets in Great Britain. Start of the Battle of Britain.
August 23	First Luftwaffe bombing raid against London.
Aug. 25 to Sep. 4	Five British retaliation attacks against Berlin.
September 4	Hitler promises to "eradicate" British cities.
September	In the "London Blitz," 5,300 tons of high-explosive bombs and 7,429 canisters of incendiaries are dropped on the city in September.
Nov. 14/15	449 German bombers attack Coventry, causing 554 civilian deaths.

Goebbels coins the new verb "*coventrieren*" (to eradicate a city by bombing).

1941

March 12	First raid on Germany by four-engined bombers (Halifax).
May 10/11	The Luftwaffe attacks London with 500 bombers, killing 1,212 civilians.
June 22	Hitler attacks the Soviet Union with an army of three million men, ending the danger of a German invasion of Britain.
June to November	Bomber Command launches relatively ineffective raids on German cities such as Berlin, Cologne, Duisburg, Düsseldorf, Hannover, Hamburg, and Mannheim. More Bomber Command crew are lost than civilians killed on the ground.
Aug. '40 to Oct. '41	In the Battle of Britain, the Luftwaffe loses 2,402 aircraft with most of their crews; 41,294 civilians are killed on the ground.
December 11	Germany declares war on the United States.

1942

February 14	The British War Cabinet orders Bomber Command to launch concentrated air attacks against German civilians, "focused on the morale of the enemy civil population and in particular of the industrial workers … The aiming points are to be the built-up areas, not, for example, dockyards or aircraft factories." [*Toronto Star*, January 8, 1945, cited in

Dan McCaffery, *Dad's War*, p. 69.]

February 22   Air Vice Marshal Arthur T. Harris becomes head of Bomber Command.

March 28/29   Lübeck is attacked by 234 aircraft, the first instance of carpet bombing by Bomber Command. Twelve bombers are lost, 320 civilians killed. Four weeks later, an operation against Rostock by 521 bombers, lasting four consecutive nights, destroys 40 percent of the city's historic built-up area.

May 30/31   Operation Millennium: the inner city of Cologne is attacked by 1,000 bombers dropping 1,455 tons of explosives and incendiaries.

July 24 to 30   Operation Gomorrha against Hamburg: the heaviest bombardment ever launched against a city, flown by 2,353 heavy bombers dropping 9,000 tons of high explosives and incendiaries. In four days, 30,500 civilians died. Including earlier and later bombing raids, a total of 55,000 civilians died in Hamburg.

1943

Jan. 31 to Feb. 2   The remnants of Germany's 6th Army surrender at Stalingrad.

March 30/31   Raid against Nuremberg by 795 aircraft dropping 2,460 tons of bombs. A total of 106 Allied aircraft are lost, and 71 are heavily damaged. Of the 545 Allied airmen who die, 112 are Canadian.

June 10   First U.S. Army Air Force raids on targets in Germany.

September 29	Italy surrenders to the Allies.
October 8 to 14	"Black Week" for the U.S. Army Air Force, which loses 148 bombers, mostly Boeing B-17s ("Flying Fortresses").

1944

May 12	Small attack against Chemnitz causes minor damage.
June 6	"D-Day," the Allied invasion in Normandy.
June 12/13	First German V-1 (rocket-propelled flying bombs, "buzz bombs") launched against London.
June 29	First heavy bombing attack against Chemnitz.
July 20	Failed attempt on Hitler's life by the German resistance.
July and August	The British Joint Intelligence Committee coins the code name *Thunderclap* for a massive operation against Berlin, envisaging up to 275,000 civilian casualties.
September 8	First V-2 bombs launched against England.
September 11	Chemnitz is attacked again; 110 civilian deaths.

1945

January 16	371 Bomber Command aircraft attack Magdeburg. [In addition to the few examples cited here, virtually all German cities were being heavily bombed throughout 1944 and the first four months of 1945.]
January 27	Harris is instructed to put Operation Thunderclap into effect, redirected against East German cities other than Berlin.

February 6	Bombing raid on Chemnitz, causing 454 civilian deaths.
February 13/14	Major Allied operation against Dresden by Bomber Command (797 Lancasters, 9 Mosquitoes) and the U.S. Army Air Force (311 B-17s) dropping 2,249 tons of high explosives and incendiaries on the historic centre of the city, killing an estimated 40,000 civilians.
February 14/15	Chemnitz is attacked by Bomber Command (with 717 bombers) and the U.S. Army Air Force (with about 150 bombers), causing 342 civilian deaths. Canadian bombers drop 431,000 pounds of incendiaries and 291,000 pounds of high explosives.
February 15/16	Bomber Command attacks Dresden again with 244 bombers.
March 2	U.S. Army Air Force attacks Dresden again, sinking a hospital ship.
March 2/3	U.S. Army Air Force attacks Chemnitz, causing 570 civilian deaths.
March 5/6	Major attack on Chemnitz by Bomber Command (760 aircraft, including 198 Canadian) and the U.S. Army Air Force, causing 2,105 civilian deaths as well as the death of 90 Canadian airmen.
April 12	Allied air attack on Chemnitz with minor forces.
April 17	572 American Flying Fortresses attack Dresden again.
April 30	Adolf Hitler commits suicide in Berlin.
May 8	Germany's unconditional surrender to the Western Allies. End of World War II in Europe.

Losses of Bomber Command Aircraft and Crew Resulting from the Operation Against Chemnitz on March 5/6, 1945

Aircraft Lost: 40 (*19 from RCAF squadrons, 21 from other squadrons*)

Killed from 6 Group:	RCAF	RAF				Total
	79	10				89

Killed from other Groups:	RCAF	RAF	RAAF	RNZA	FFFAF	Total
	11	51	10	4	7	83

Total Killed	RCAF	RAF	RAAF	RNZA	FFFAF	Total
	90	61	10	4	7	172

POW:	RCAF	RAF		RNZA		Total
	30	16		1		47

The author has compiled a complete list of the 40 Bomber Command aircraft lost, the 172 crew members killed and the 47 crew members taken POW in this operation. The list shows A/C number, squadron number, cause and location of crash (if known), names and ranks of crew members and their national air force affiliation (RCAF, RAF, RAAF, RNZAF, FFAF). The list can be e-mailed upon request. Please contact the author: p.hessel@sympatico.ca.

Note: The list does not include losses suffered by the U.S. Army Air Force in this joint operation.

Canadian Airmen Murdered in the Last Year of World War II

1. Chronological listing of 25 Canadian airmen murdered on German and German-occupied territory between July 1944 and April 1945, based on the German Web site www.flieger-lynchmorde.de. The list is incomplete. Its author, Willi Wachholz of Schwerte, Germany, was expecting further reports.

July 26, 1944: Murder of a Canadian airman in Oberweier (now part of Gaggenau). Source: *Badische Neueste Nachrichten,* May 30, May 31, and June 1, 1991.

August 1944(?): Murder of an unknown Canadian airman in Klein Flöthe (Altenröder Holz) by members of *"Heimatschutz"* [Home Guard]. Now, Klein Flöthe belongs to the municipality of Oderwald, District of Wolfenbüttel. Source: Reinhard Försterling et al, *1200 Jahre Gross Flöthe, Eine Chronik* [1,200 Years of Klein Flöthe], 1988, p. 90.

Fall of 1944 (probably September): Murder of two Canadian airmen by a Luftwaffe officer who was head of a training camp, at a glider port near Giessen. Source: Letter from an eyewitness, October 5, 2001.

Fall of 1944: Murder of an unknown Canadian airman in Steinbach near Giessen by a teacher and his class of students. Source: Richard Humphrey, Rolf Haaser, Miriam Pagenkemper (editors), *Der Untergang des alten Giessen* [The Destruction of Old Giessen] (Giessen: 1994), p. 47.

Fall of 1944: Murder of an unknown Allied airman (probably a Canadian) on the road to Kemel (now belonging to the municipality of Heidenrod) by the village policeman. Source: Letter from an eyewitness of November 11, 2002, and an e-mail dated November 13, 2002.

September 12, 1944: Murder of a Canadian officer (pilot in the USAAF) in Bingen by members of the SA and the Nazi Party district office. Sources: *Neuer Mainzer Anzeiger,* June 15, 1946; letter from an eyewitness of November 28, 2000; Marie-Christine Werner, *Der englische Flieger: Der Mord an Cyril William Sibley* [The English Airman: Murder of Cyril William Sibley], a radio program of *Südwestrundfunk* in Mainz on February 10, 2001, transcript, p. 37.

October 28, 1944: Murder of a Canadian airman in Haltern (Helenenhöhe). Source: Peter Krone, *Historische Dokumentation "Hingerichtetengräber" auf dem Friedhof Wehl in Hameln* [Historical documentation of the graves of executed persons at the Wehl cemetery in Hameln] (Hameln: 1987), p. 77.

November 5, 1944: Murder of four Canadian airmen (prisoners of war) in Solingen by SA men. Sources: *Rhein-Echo,* June 4,

1947, and *Rheinische Post*, June 7, 1947. Bundesarchiv [Federal Archives], Koblenz: *Akte All Prov. 8, JAG 248.*

December 24, 1944: Murder of two RAF airmen, the British pilot Hislop and the Canadian Lindenboom in Uerdingen and Stratum (today parts of Krefeld) by a Wehrmacht corporal and an SS man, respectively. Both airmen were crew members in a British bomber. Source: Dieter Hangebruch, "Die Beschuldigten sind tot: Zwei Fälle von Lynchjustiz an alliierten Fliegern bei Uerdingen 1944" [The accused are dead: Two lynchings of Allied airmen near Uerdingen in 1944], 10-page typescript. Was to be published in Krefeld in 2003 in a yearbook called *Heimat* [Homeland].

January 1, 1945: Murder of a Canadian airman near Loccum by members of an SS command headquarters. Sources: War chronicle by the Lutheran congregation of Loccum (Parish Archives) by Pastor Christoph Schomerius, 1945; Konrad Droste, *Loccum: Ein Dorf, Das Kloster, Der Wald. Beiträge zu einer bemerkenswerten Ortsgeschichte* [Loccum: a village, the monastery, the forest. Noteworthy historical observations] (Rehburg-Loccum: 1999), p. 104. Bundesarchiv, Koblenz: *Akte All Prov. 8, JAG 351.*

January 7, 1945: Murder of a Canadian air force officer by a Wehrmacht soldier in Hanau. Source: *Hanauer Anzeiger*, February 19, March 10, and March 11, 1953.

March 1945: Murder of the Canadian pilot of a fighter bomber, Lieutenant Georg Kienzle, at the Deiningen airfield near Nördlingen by a Luftwaffe ground crew soldier. Source: Letter from an eyewitness of October 9, 2001 (including diary pages).

March 6, 1945: Murder of the Canadian airman R.B. Denison [actually Pilot Officer Jean Maurice D'Avril] in Frankenberg/ Saxony by civilians.[1] Source: Manfred Ahnert, *Tod des abgeschossenen kanadischen Bomberpiloten* [Death of the crashed Canadian bomber pilot] (Frankenberg: 2001), six-page typescript in the Frankenberg town archives.

March 8, 1945: Murder of a Canadian airman in Schlossvippach and a British airman in Vippachedelhausen by the district administrator [*Landrat*] of Weimar District, who had already shot and killed five American airman with his "followers" on July 29, 1944 in Ottmannshausen. Sources: Thüringen State Archives [*Hauptstaatsarchiv*] in Weimar, *Akte Kreisrat Weimar, Nr. 1079*, letter by the mayor of Schlossvippach dated March 15, 1946; letter by a local historian, dated January 21, 2001, based on eyewitness reports.

March 16, 1945: Murder of two Canadian airmen near Altenau — now belonging to the municipality of Oberharz — by two Gestapo men. Sources: Peter Krone, *Historische Dokumentation "Hingerichtetengräber" auf dem Friedhof Wehl in Hameln*, 1987, p. 83; Letter from the Municipality of Oberharz dated November 16, 2000.

March 25, 1945: Murder of two Canadian and one English [actually all three were RCAF] airmen in the Wulfen district of Dorsten. Source: Letter from the Dorsten town archives, dated November 10, 2000.[2]

April 1945: Murder of an unknown Canadian airman in Dux, in the then Protectorate of Bohemia and Moravia (today called Duchcov, Czech Republic). Source: Letter from an eyewitness, dated January 24, 2002.

April 3, 1945: Murder of a Canadian airman by Gestapo men in Hagen. Sources: *Westfälische Rundschau,* No. 53, Hagen, September 18, 1946; Peter Krone, *Historische Dokumentation "Hingerichtetengräber" auf dem Friedhof Wehl in Hameln,* 1987, p. 72; Gerhard E. Sollbach, (ed.), *Hagen: Kriegsjahre und Nachkriegszeit, 1939–1948* [Hagen: War Years and Post-War Years, 1939–1948], 3rd edition (Hagen: 1995), p. 26; Ralf Blank, *Die Endphase und das Chaos. In: Hagen unterm Hakenkreuz* [The End Phase and Chaos, in *Hagen under the Swastika*]
(Hagen: 1995), p. 367; Bundesarchiv, Koblenz: *Akte All Prov. 8, JAG 202; Justiz und NS-Verbrechen* [Justice and Nazi Crimes], a collection of German criminal judgements pertaining to Nazi murders, 1945–1966, in *"Seminarium voor Strafrecht en Strafrechtspleging Van Hamel,"* University of Amsterdam, vol. X (Amsterdam: 1973), pp. 5–9.

April 25, 1945: Murder of an unknown Canadian airman on the island of Wangerooge by a member of the German Navy. Source: Hans-Jürgen Jürgens, *Zeugnisse aus unheilvoller Zeit: Ein Kriegstagebuch über die Ereignisse 1939–1945 im Bereich Wangerooge, Spiekeroog, Langeoog sowie die Lage im Reich und an den Fronten* [Witness to an evil time: A war diary pertaining to events from 1939 to 1945 in the Wangerooge, Spiekeroog, Langeoog region ...], 5th edition (Jever: 1991), pp. 605 and 614.

2. In addition to the above list, I have found evidence of the following murders, bringing the total to at least 37 and possibly 44 between July 1944 and April 1945. It is reasonable to expect that more murders occurred during that period which are not recorded in the above list and which have not come my attention either.

July 11, 1944: Murder of RCAF F/Lt James Dale in Luden-hausen. He was shot by Karl Stern, a forest warden, who had been a flyer in World War I and had suffered a head wound. Dale was buried at the cemetery in Ludenhausen. Source: www.ludenhausen.de/chronik_st1.htm.

March 1945: Six RCAF airmen were murdered at the Sagan *Stalag* (see page 106 of this text).

March 6, 1945: At least one, possibly more, Canadian airmen were murdered in the Humboldthöhe neighbourhood of Chemnitz, by unknown persons.

March 22, 1945: The author has also learned that the following three Canadian airmen were executed by Volkssturm men after their Lancaster was shot down near Opladen: F/Lt James Frederick Hadley, F/O Daniel Frame, and F/Sgt John MacKenzie (all from 428 Squadron). Karl Schaefer was sentenced to 15 years in prison for his connection with the shooting.[3]

NOTES

Chapter 1

1. DND Directorate of History and Heritage, file 285 F I, p. 47.
2. Later, at Library and Archives Canada, on Wellington Street in Ottawa, I learned that this unit with the long-winded name, abbreviated as CWCIU, had been established at the request of Canadian Military Headquarters (the forerunner of the Department of National Defence) effective June 4, 1945, less than a month after the end of the war in Europe. The unit consisted of 16 officers (three colonels, five majors, three captains, and five lieutenants) and 14 other ranks. It was divided into two sections: one was stationed in London, while the other travelled throughout "Northwest Europe" including Germany. Perhaps due to the rapidly changing political climate, the unit had only a short life. It concerned itself mainly with the prosecution of SS *Brigadeführer* Kurt Meyer, who was held responsible for the execution of Canadian soldiers in Normandy.
3. Karen Loofs, Senior Research Coordinator, Department of Justice Canada.

Chapter 2

1. Dave McIntosh, *Terror in the Starboard Sea* (Don Mills: General Publishing, 1980).
2. "Immediate equipment" was 18 bombers (two flights of 9); "extended equipment" was up to 25 bombers. Dr Steve Harris, DND Archives, conversation with author.
3. Leslie Hannon, *Canada at War*. (Toronto: McClelland & Stewart, 1968), p. 96.
4. J.L. Granatstein and Desmond Morton, *Canada and the Two World Wars* (Toronto: Key Porter Books, 2003), p. 249.
5. Sir Arthur Harris, *Bomber Offensive* (London: Collins, 1947), p. 134.
6. *The Canadian Encyclopedia*, 2nd edition (Edmonton: Hurtig, 1988); p. 595; Christian Zentner, (ed.), *Der Zweite Weltkrieg, ein Lexikon* [World War II Lexicon] (Vienna: Tosa Edition, 2004), p. 144.
7. Goddard Lance, *D-Day Juno Beach: Canada's 24 Hours of Destiny* (Toronto: Dundurn, 2004), p. 221.
8. Charles Messenger, *"Bomber" Harris and the Strategic Bombing Offensive, 1939–1945*. (London: Arms and Armour Press, 1984), p. 185.
9. Frederick Taylor, *Dresden, Tuesday, February 13, 1945*, pp. 168 and 467.
10. Ibid., p. 186.
11. Martin Middlebrook and Chris Everitt, *Bomber Command War Diaries,1939–1945* (London: Viking, 1985), p. 663. Robin Neillands, *The Bomber War: The Allied Air Offensive Against Nazi Germany*. (New York: Overlook, 2003), p. 351, attributes this sentence to Air Marshal Sir Norman Bottomley, Deputy Chief of Air Staff, addressed to Sir Arthur Harris on January 27, 1945.
12. John H. McQuiston, *Tannoy Calling* (New York: Vantage Press, 1990), p. xi.

13. DND Directorate of History and Heritage, file 181.003 (D 792), Bomber Command Interpretations, Report K 3899, *Target Chemnitz, 17 February to 15 March 1945*.

14. Taylor, *Dresden*, p. 337.

15. Library and Archives Canada, Acc. no. 1996-212, Album Call no. 86/146.

16. Taylor. *Dresden*, p. 336ff.

17. DND Directorate of History and Heritage, file 181.003 (D 792), Bomber Command Interpretations, Report K 3899, *Target Chemnitz, 17 February to 15 March 1945*, file 181.003 (D 1770), Immediate Interpretation, Report K 3767, *Chemnitz*.

18. Laurence Motiuk, *Thunderbirds at War*(Ottawa: Larmot Associates, 1998), p. 444.

19. David Brown, *The History of Air Warfare* (London: Guinness Superlatives, 1976), p. 154.

Chapter 3

1. Library and Archives Canada, RG 24, vol. 28738, in file "Stillinger, Roy Edward," Post Presumption Memorandum no. 1104/48. W.H. Denison's service number: R 271724.

Chapter 4

1. Frankenberg was an important garrison town during the *Kaiserreich* (the old Empire), the Weimar Republic, and the Nazi period. In 1945, the large complex of barracks was called the *Hindenburg Kaserne* and was occupied by units of the Red Army. Later, it housed troops of the GDR's *Volksarmee*. See the commemorative brochure by Holger Hase, *Tag des offenen Denkmals 2003 in Frankenberg, Zur Geschichte der Frankenberger Garnison*.

Chapter 5

1. Commonwealth War Graves Commission, Ottawa, August 2004, faxed information.

2. Motiuk. *Thunderbirds at War*, p. 460.

3. Glenn Matthews of Victoria, B.C., July 8, 2004, e-mail received by author.

4. DND Archives, 181.003 D 1136.

5. W. Rodney, *Deadly Mission: Canadian Airmen Over Nuremberg, March 1944* (Ottawa: CEF Books, 2001), p. 38.

6. Christian Zentner. *Der Zweite Weltkrieg, ein Lexikon*, p. 404.

7. Kenneth Blyth, *Cradle Crew: Royal Canadian Air Force, World War II* (Manhattan, Kansas: Sunflower University Press, 1997), pp. 104–105.

8. DND Directorate of History and Heritage, file 181.003 (D 792), Bomber Command Interpretations, Report K 3899, *Target Chemnitz, 17 February to 15 March 1945*.

9. Library and Archives Canada LAC RG 24, vol. 27873, file J. Kastner, J-94419.

10. Library and Archives Canada LAC RG 24, vol. 28555, file R.D. Ross, J-8165.

11. Library and Archives Canada LAC RG 24, vol. 25025, file A. Cash, J-38805. RCAF Casualty Enquiry No. G (P 430150-45)

12. Library and Archives Canada LAC RG 24, vol. 28555, file R.D. Ross, J-8165.

Chapter 6

1. *Bomben auf Chemnitz* (Chemnitz: Schlossbergmuseum, 1995).

2. Elfriede Adamietz, in Karin Fahnert, *Chemnitzer Erinnerungen 1945*, pp. 11–12.

3. *Chemnitzer Zeitung*, January 19 to May 6, 1945, Stadtarchiv Chemnitz, vol. 48, microfilm.

4. Pornitz/Vogel family archives, cited in Gert Richter, *Chemnitzer Erinnerungen 1945*, p. 155.

Chapter 7

1. Named after World War I General Erich Ludendorff, who became a Nazi sympathizer and marched with Hitler in the Munich "Putsch" of 1923. Immediately after the war, the street was renamed Seminarstrasse. During the GDR period, it was named after German Communist leader Ernst Thälmann, who was murdered in Buchenwald in 1944. It is now called Badstrasse again, as it was before the Nazi period.

2. Minutes of the Frankenberg Town Council, *Protokoll 43, 1945*.

3. Minutes of the Frankenberg Town Council, *Protokoll 43, 1945*. "No. 240, letter by Dr Wolff to the Mayor of Frankenberg, stamped received on September 17, 1945, decision on September 22, 1945: matter to be discussed at the council meeting."

4. No. 478, *Rat der Stadt Frankenberg, Abt. Standesamt*, file 832041, " *Kriegssterbefall-Anzeigen*," June 6, 1945 to December 1973.

5. Rossberg's memoirs had come to the attention of Dr Koch in Berlin, who in turn told the author about the murder of the unknown Canadian airman.

Chapter 9

1. Greenhous, Brereton, et al, *The RCAF Overseas*, p. 859.

2. Kurt Pätzold, "Grosse Woche [Big Week]," an article in *Junge Welt*, April 3/5, 2004 (No. 78).

3. Christian Zentner, (ed.). *Der Zweite Weltkrieg, ein Lexikon*, p. 190.

4. Avalon Project at Yale Law School, "Nazi Conspiracy and Aggression," vol. 2, chapter XVI, part 4, www.yale.edu/lawweb/avalon/imt/document/nca …

5. Günter Assmann, Strasse der Befreiung 13, D-09599 Freiberg, Germany.

6. Philip Kaplan, *Round the Clock.* (New York: Random House, 1993), p. 193ff.

7. W.R. Chorley, *Bomber Command Losses of the Second World War, vol. 6, 1945* (Leicester: Midland Publishing Co.: 1998).

8. Richard Reiter, cited by George Gamester, *Toronto Star*, January 23, 1997, p. A4.

Chapter 10

1. Philip Roth, *The Human Stain* (New York: Vintage Press), p. 344.

Chapter 11

1. Library and Archives Canada, LAC RG 24, file 54383.

2. Library and Archives Canada, LAC RG 24, file 00-54383.

3. This letter was addressed only to Mr. Henri D'Avril, although "his family" was mentioned in the last sentence. Did casualty officers in the late 1940s know nothing about a mother's pain who has lost her only son? Did they solely rely on the "head of the family" to convey the message to his wife? Were there RCAF regulations that specified how to address and write such letters? Compared with the unwillingness or reluctance of Canadian defence authorities to

investigate the death of a young Canadian, a death that should have raised suspicion at some level, it seems like a very minor error that the location of the cemetery where D'Avril was "laid to rest" was given as "eight miles east from the centre of Berlin", when it is about three miles (five kilometres) west of the centre, in the western suburb of Charlottenburg, in what was then the British sector of the divided city. Had the cemetery been eight miles east of the centre, it would have been in the Soviet sector (and later inside the German Democratic Republic). Another error in Gunn's letter was the statement that "his crewmates lie at rest beside him in adjacent graves". This is not the case. While the other two crew members who died are buried in the same cemetery, their "resting places" are in different plots: D'Avril is in Plot 13 Row C, Grave 7. Pilot Officer Desbien is in Plot 8, Row C, Grave 7, and Flight Sergeant Minguet is in Plot 2, Row C, Grave 12.

Chapter 12

1. Greenhous, Brereton, et al, p. 133ff. According to Spencer Dunmore et al, *Reap the Whirlwind: The Untold Story of Six Group, Canada's Bomber Force of World War II* (Toronto: McClelland & Stewart, 1991), p. 351, 760 aircraft took off to attack Chemnitz, including 185 from Six Group.This total included the Pathfinders.
2. Halifax Aircraft Association, *The Halifax — a living memorial to our past* (Toronto).
3. According to www.rcaf.com/6group/425.html, Lecomte was commander only until August 20, 1944, succeeded by H. Ledoux (August 21, 1944, to June 10, 1945). The last page of Joe Parent's own log book is signed by H. Leroux, Commanding Officer, 425 (RCAF) Squadron, on March 7, 1945.
4. The corkscrew was an evasive manoeuvre. As soon as a gunner warned of an impending attack by a fighter, the pilot had to turn sharply and simultaneously dive towards the approaching fighter, then quickly reverse direction while pulling the aircraft up into a steep climb. See W. Rodney, *Deadly Mission*, p. 15, and Dan McCaffery, *Dad's War*, p. 67.
5. The German night fighters had developed twin upward-firing cannons mounted behind the cockpit. The pilot fired with the aid of a reflector sight, enabling the crew to attack the bomber's blind spot under the fuselage. The Germans called this deadly device "*schräge Musik*" [slanted music]. Philip Kaplan, p. 183

Chapter 13

1. It may have been a village near Annaberg, since in 1945 the town of Annaberg had a population of about 30,000.
2. It is possible that Leo Lamontagne was wounded during this attack.

Chapter 14

1. The *Heimbürgerin* (literally, home citizen) was a village woman who washed and prepared the dead before burial.
2. Documents indicate that the bodies were probably removed on or about March 7; they were buried at Drebach cemetery on March 11, 1945.
3. On March 30, the Mayor of Drebach wrote that it would present great difficulty and take a

long time to move the wreckage to the Army maintenance yard in Oschatz, and that he had now withdrawn the guard from the crash site.

4.   The Ore Mountains are famous for folk art products, especially handmade wooden Christmas decorations.

5.   Later, I sent a fax with some crude drawings of the bolt to Bill Tytula of the Halifax project at the RCAF Museum in Trenton. He confirmed that it was a stainless steel pivot bolt from an axle arrangement in the landing gear of the Halifax.

Chapter 15

1.   Lise never lost contact with Margot Chayer, who, sadly, is too ill to speak to me or to comprehend the significance of my discovery. Margot mourned for Jean-Maurice most of her life and only married when she was in her sixties. Her husband died recently.

Chapter 16

1.   Dan McCaffery, *Dad's War*, page 50–51.

2.   Ibid., pp. 52ff.

Chapter 17

1.   Division of Information Processing, City of Chemnitz, March 21, 2005, statistical information given via telephone.

Chapter 18

1.   W. Rodney, *Deadly Mission: Canadian Airmen Over Nuremberg, March 1944*, pp. 1–2.

2.   Elfriede Rupprecht, Sachsenburg, August 14, 2004, letter to the author.

Appendix IV

1.   The identity of the murder victim turned out to be wrong, based on a misinterpretation of facts by German military historians. There is also evidence that the "civilians" who committed the murder were in fact Nazi officials.

2.   The murder victims — all three were RCAF from Halifax III *MZ-907* coded *6U-P*, of 415 Squadron, shot down by flak during an attack on Münster — were Pilot Officer R.A. Paul, Pilot Officer J.M. Jones, and Pilot Officer L.W. Brennan. Their graves were found in the Kusenhorst Forest, and moved to the Canadian War Cemetery in Groesbeek, Netherlands. The Canadians were shot by *Haupttruppenführer* Ferdinand Assmann, who was later arrested and committed suicide while in prison awaiting trial. W.R.Chorley, *Bomber Command Losses of the Second World War* (March 25, 1945).

3.   Library and Archives Canada, RG-24, file 27539 (Frame); RG-24, file 27661 (Hadley); RG-24, file 28103 (MacKenzie).

BIBLIOGRAPHY

Works Cited

Allison, Les, and Harry Haywood. *They Shall Grow Not Old: A Book of Remembrance.* Brandon, MN: Commonwealth Air Training Plan Museum, 1991.

Blyth, Kenneth K. *Cradle Crew: Royal Canadian Air Force, World War II.* Manhattan, KS: Sunflower University Press, 1997.

Brown, David, et al. *The History of Air Warfare.* London: Guinness Superlatives,1976.

Chorley, W.R. *Bomber Command Losses of the Second World War.* Vol. 6, *1945.* Leicester: Midland Publishing Co., 1998.

Dunmore, Spencer, and William Carter. *Reap the Whirlwind: The Untold Story of Six Group, Canada's Bomber Force of World War II.* Toronto: McClelland & Stewart, 1991.

Fahnert, Karin, and Gert Richter. *Chemnitzer Erinnerungen 1945* (Reminiscences of Chemnitz in 1945). Chemnitz: Verlag Heimatland Sachsen, 1996.

Goddard, Lance. *D-Day Juno Beach: Canada's 24 Hours of Destiny.* Toronto: Dundurn, 2004.

Granatstein, J.L., and Desmond Morton. *Canada and the Two World Wars.* Toronto: Key Porter Books, 2003.

Greenhous, Brereton, Steve Harris, et al. *The Official History of the RCAF.* Vol. III, *The RCAF Overseas: The Crucible of War.* Toronto: University of Toronto Press, 1994.

Hannon, Leslie. *Canada at War.* Toronto: McClelland & Stewart, 1968.

Harris, Sir Arthur. *Bomber Offensive.* London: Collins, 1947; Canadian edition: Toronto: Stoddart, 1990.

Hase, Holger. *Geschichte der Frankenberger Garnison: Ein militär-historischer Abriss* (History of the Frankenberg Garrison: An episode of military history). Mittweida: Landratsamt, 2003.

Kaplan, Philip. *Round the Clock.* New York: Random House, 1993.

Kästner, Max. *Frankenberger Heimatbuch: Aus dem Leben einer kleinen Stadt.* (A Local History of Frankenberg: From the life of a small town). Frankenberg: C. G. Rossberg, 1938.

McCaffery, Dan. *Dad's War.* Toronto: James Lorimer, 2004.

McIntosh, Dave. *Terror in the Starboard Seat.* Don Mills: General Publishing, 1980.

McQuiston, John H. *Tannoy Calling: A Story of Canadian Airmen Flying against Nazi Germany.* New York: Vantage Press, 1990.

Messenger, Charles. *"Bomber" Harris and the Strategic Bombing Offensive, 1939–1945.* London: Arms and Armour Press, 1984.

Middlebrook, Martin, and Chris Everitt. *Bomber Command War Diaries, 1939–1945.* London: Viking, 1985.

Motiuk, Laurence. *Thunderbirds at War: Diary of a Bomber Squadron.* Nepean: Larmot, 1998.

Neillands, Robin. *The Bomber War: The Allied Air Offensive Against Nazi Germany.* New York: Overlook, 2003.

Peden, Murray. *A Thousand Shall Fall.* Stittsville, ON: Canada's Wings, 1979.

Richter, Gert. *Chemnitzer Erinnerungen 1945* (Reminiscences of Chemnitz in 1945). Chemnitz: Verlag Heimatland Sachsen, 2001.

Rodney, W. *Deadly Mission: Canadian Airmen Over Nuremberg, March 1944.* Ottawa: CEF Books, 2001.

Rossberg, Johannes, et al. *Frankenberg im Jahre 1945* (Frankenberg in 1945). Frankenberg: Rossberg, 2002.

Roth, Philip. *The Human Stain.* New York: Vintage Press, 2001.

Taylor, Frederick. *Dresden, Tuesday, February 13, 1945.* New York: Harper Collins, 2004.

Zentner, Christian, ed. *Der Zweite Weltkrieg, ein Lexikon* (World War II Lexicon).Vienna: Tosa Edition, 2004.

Further Reading

Avalon Project. *Charter of the International Military Tribunal.* Yale University, 1996.

Barker, Ralph. *Strike Hard, Strike Sure: Epics of the Bombers.* London: Chatto & Windus, 1963.

Bingham, Victor. *Halifax — Second to None: The Handley Page Halifax.* Shrewsbury, England: Airlife, 1986.

Bomben auf Chemnitz. Chemnitz: Schlossbergmuseum, 1995.

Boog, Horst. *Der anglo-amerikanische Luftkrieg über Europa und die deutsche Luftverteidigung:* Das Deutsche Reich und der Zweite Weltkrieg, vol. 6 (Der globale Krieg), pp. 429–560. Stuttgart: 1990.

Bowyer, Chaz. *Tales from the Bombers.* London: William Kimber, 1985.

Brockhaus Enzyklopädie. Wiesbaden: Brockhaus, 1974.

Dancocks, Daniel G. *In Enemy Hands: Canadian Prisoners of War, 1939–1945.* Edmonton: Hurtig, 1983.

Fiedler, Uwe. *Bomben auf Chemnitz.* Chemnitz: Verlag Heimatland, 2005.

Friedrich, Jörg. *Der Brand : Deutschland im Bombenkrieg 1940–1945* (The Conflagration: Germany in the bombing war, 1940–1945). Munich: Propyläen-Verlag, 2002.

Friedrich, Jörg. *Brandstätten: Der Anblick des Bombenkrieges* (Burned Places: The face of the bombing war). Munich: Propyläen-Verlag, 2003.

Grayling, A.C. *The Meaning of Things.* London: Phoenix, 2002.

Grayling, A.C. *The Reason of Things.* London: Phoenix, 2003.

Groehler, Olaf: *Bombenkrieg gegen Deutschland,* Berlin: 1990.

Gurney, Gene. *The War in the Air: A Pictorial History of World War II Air Forces in Combat.* New York: Crown, 1962.

Howard, Michael, et al. *The Laws of War: Constraints on Warfare in the Western World.* Yale University: 1994.

Irving, David. *The Destruction of Dresden.* London: Focal Point, 1963.

Jablonski, Edward. *Flying Fortress.* New York: Doubleday, 1965.

Knell, Hermann. *To Destroy a City.* Cambridge, Mass.: 2003.

Kucklick, Christoph. *Der Feuersturm — Bombenkrieg über*

Deutschland. Hamburg: Ellert + Richter, 2003.

Longmate, Norman. *The Bombers: The RCAF Offensive Against Germany, 1939–1945.* London: Hutchinson, 1983.

Mackprang Baer, Gertrud. *In the Shadow of Silence.* Toronto: Harper Collins, 2002.

Matas, David. *Justice Delayed: Nazi War Criminals in Canada.* Toronto: Summerhill Press, 1987.

McCaffery, Dan. *Battlefields in the Air: Canadians in the Allied Bomber Command.* Toronto: James Lorimer, 1995.

McKee, Alexander. *Dresden 1945: The Devil's Tinderbox.* London: Souvenir Press, 1982.

Milberry, Larry, and Hugh Halliday. *The Royal Canadian Air Force at War, 1939–1945.* Toronto: CANAV Books, 1990.

OHCHR: Office of the High Commission on Human Rights. *The Geneva Convention Relative to the Treatment of Prisoners of War.* 1949. www.unhchr.ch/html/menu3/b/91.htm.

Report by the Supreme Commander to the Combined Chiefs of Staff on the Operations in Europe of the Allied Expeditionary Force, 6 June 1944 to 8 May 1945. London: 1946.

Rolfe, Mel. *Looking Into Hell.* London: Rigel Edition, 2004.

Rossberg, Johannes, et al. *Max-Kästner-Strasse, Dr-Wilhelm-Külz-Strasse.* Frankenberg: 2002.

Rumpf, Hans. *The Bombing of Germany.* London: Frederick Muller Limited, 1963.

Sorge, Martin K. *The Other Price of Hitler's War: German Military and Civilian Losses Resulting from World War II.* Westport, Connecticut: Greenwood Press, 1986.

Snyder, Louis L. *Encyclopedia of the Third Reich.* New York: Paragon, 1989.

Target Germany. London: Cavendish House, 1974.

United States Air Force. *Intelligence Targeting Guide, Air Force Pamphlet 14–210 Intelligence.* 1996. www.fas.org/irp/doddir/usaf/afpam14-210/part20.htm#page180.

Verrier, Anthony. *The Bomber Offensive.* London: Batsford, 1968.

Vonnegut, Kurt. *Slaughterhouse-Five.* New York: Random House, 1969.

Wainwright, John. *Tail-End Charlie: One Man's Journey Through War.* London: MacMillan, 1978.

Walther, Manfred. *Bomben auf Harthau.* Chemnitz: Heimat-sammlung Harthau, 2004.

Webster, Sir Charles, and Noble Frankland. *The Strategic Air Offensive Against Germany 1939–1945.* 4 Vols. London: HM Stationary Office, 1961.

PHOTO CREDITS

INDEX